S0-DFK-764

Circle Time
Math

Written by Susan Finkel
and Karen Seberg

Illustrated by Gary Mohrman

Teaching & Learning Company

1204 Buchanan St., P.O. Box 10
Carthage, IL 62321

This book belongs to

_____

The activity portrayed on the front cover is described on page 88.

Cover by Gary Mohrman

Copyright © 1996, Teaching & Learning Company

ISBN No. 1-57310-064-1

Printing No. 987654321

Teaching & Learning Company
1204 Buchanan St., P.O. Box 10
Carthage, IL 62321

The purchase of this book entitles teachers to make copies for use in their individual classrooms only. This book, or any part of it, may not be reproduced in any form for any other purposes without prior written permission from the Teaching & Learning Company. It is strictly prohibited to reproduce any part of this book for an entire school or school district, or for commercial resale.

All rights reserved. Printed in the United States of America.

Table of Contents

TLC10064 Copyright © Teaching & Learning Company, Carthage, IL 62321

Table of Math Processes

Every reasonable attempt has been made to identify copyrighted material.

TLC10064 Copyright © Teaching & Learning Company, Carthage, IL 62321

Dear Teacher or Parent,

How often have you said these words *OK, everyone, time for circle time. Let's gather on the rug!* and then thought to yourself "What should we do today?" This book will help you through those times when you are tired of the same old ideas. We've taken many familiar children's songs and created some great circle time activities for you to try. In addition, we'll give you ideas for originating your own songs, using these familiar tunes.

What is circle time?
Circle times are large or small group gatherings. During your circle time, you may present daily or weekly themes or concepts. You may use books, pictures, flannel boards, concrete materials, share experiences and sing songs!

What is the best way to do circle time?
There is no "best" way. Each teacher has his or her own style. You can gather ideas for your circle times by reading books, attending classes and observing other teachers. Eventually, you will develop your own style that works best for you and your class. Be aware that you may need to adjust your style from year to year, or even as the school year progresses, depending on the changes in your children.

Some circle time hints:
Establish a set place in your classroom to gather. It should be out of the room's main traffic pattern. A round or oval rug makes a great visual cue for the children as they come together. If possible, locate your circle time space near a window.

Have an easel, chalkboard or flannel board nearby for using visual aids or recording the children's ideas.

If you prefer a "backup" when you sing, use a tape, CD or record player. You don't need to be a great singer to have great circle times, but you will need to know how to use this equipment.

Plan your circle times for the same time each day. Children need a consistent schedule for each day's activities; they feel security in knowing the sequence of a day's planned events. Create a consistent pattern of activities within your circle time as well.

Name your circle time whatever you wish: morning meeting, group time, together time or something else unique to your children.

Use concrete items whenever possible.

If you find the children are not responding to a particular activity or song, STOP. Try again later on another day or in another way.

Sincerely,

Susan Karen

Susan Finkel and Karen Seberg

TLC10064 Copyright © Teaching & Learning Company, Carthage, IL 62321

About This Book

Math is more than just adding, subtracting, multiplying and dividing. Today's children need to be exposed to mathematical concepts at at an early age. How can we prepare them for these experiences? Before children are ready to add or subtract (or eventually complete algebraic computations), there are a number of math processes that are the basis for understanding. These processes or building blocks are:

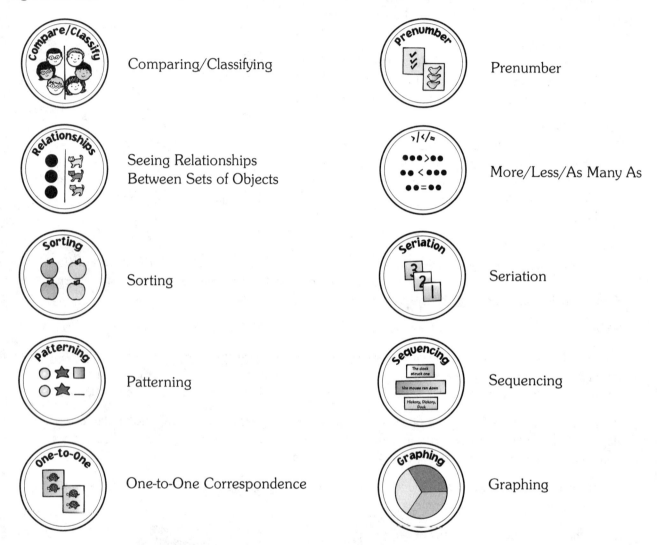

Comparing/Classifying

Prenumber

Seeing Relationships Between Sets of Objects

More/Less/As Many As

Sorting

Seriation

Patterning

Sequencing

One-to-One Correspondence

Graphing

Children need a variety of experiences with these processes before they can be successful with addition, subtraction or other math skills.

The circle times in this book give children those experiences using familiar children's songs as a basis for the activities. You will find that these processes are interrelated and flow together. It may be hard to distinguish where "seeing relationships" ends and where "comparing" begins or how "classifying" and "sorting" differ from each other. What is important is to give the children an opportunity to explore and experience these basic processes and form their own natural and relevant connections.

For more information on math processes, skills and developmentally appropriate activities for preschool children, here are some resources:

Baratta-Lorton, Mary. *Mathematics Their Way.* Addison-Wesley, 1976.

Bredekamp, Susan (ed.) *Developmentally Appropriate Practice in Early Childhood Programs Serving Children from Birth Through Age Eight* (expanded edition). NAEYC, 1987.

Miller, Karen. *Ages & Stages.* Telshare Publishing Co., 1985.

TLC10064 Copyright © Teaching & Learning Company, Carthage, IL 62321

The Ants Go Marching

The ants go marching one by one,
Hurrah! Hurrah!
The ants go marching one by one,
Hurrah! Hurrah!
The ants go marching one by one,
The little one stops to suck his thumb,
And they all go marching down
To the ground, to get out of the rain,
Boom, boom, boom.
(verses)
two by two; tie his shoe.
three by three; climb a tree.
four by four; shut the door.
five by five; scratch his thigh.
six by six; pick up sticks
seven by seven; go to heaven
eight by eight; shut the gate
nine by nine; said, "I'm behind!"
ten by ten; said, "This is the end!"

Compare/Classify

Props/Visual Aids

Reproduce the ant and anthill patterns on page 10. Make cards showing five ants and one hill in each of the colors you wish to compare. Make another set of cards by reducing and enlarging the ant and hill patterns to make five small ants and a hill, five larger ants and a hill and so on.

Talk About

Mix the colored ants and hills together and spread the cards on the circle time rug. Work together to classify the ants. Say, "Let's put all the red ants in the red hill." Repeat the activity with the small and large ants and hills. "Where do you think these tiny ants live? How are these ants different? How are these the same?"

To Extend This Circle Time

Make anthills for a snack. Help the children spread peanut butter on a round or oval-shaped cracker to make the anthill. Give each child a few raisins for the ants. Enjoy your snack with glasses of cold milk!

TLC10064 Copyright © Teaching & Learning Company, Carthage, IL 62321

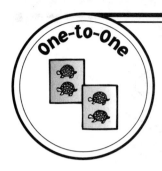

Props/Visual Aids

Give each child 10 small plastic ants (found in some board games) or 10 ant cards from the patterns on page 10. Divide the children into groups of two, and give each pair of children a drawing of the anthill (pattern on page 10).

Talk About

As you sing the song, have each child count out the number of ants in the verse. Then ask the children to match their ants with their partners' ants. Ask, "Do the ants line up exactly? Are the number of ants the same?" The children can then "march" their ants two by two, three by three and so on into the anthill.

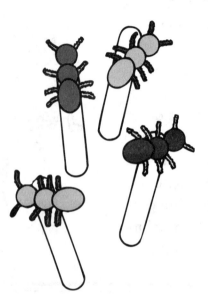

To Extend This Circle Time

Supply the art center with brown or black construction paper, safety scissors, small (3" [8 cm]) pieces of pipe cleaners, large craft sticks, glue and tape. Help the children cut two circles and one oval to glue together for the ant's body. (You may want to precut the shapes to simplify the project.) Tape two pipe cleaner pieces on the ant's head for antennae and six pipe cleaner pieces on the body for legs. Attach a large craft stick to the back of the body to make an ant stick puppet. You will have many unique ant shapes! Invite the children to march the puppets two by two (and so on) around the room. Locate an ant farm for your science center. Count the ants in the farm.

Props/Visual Aids

Place 10 plastic ants in a basket or container. You may also use the ant patterns on page 10 to make ant cards.

Talk About

Pass the basket of ants around the group of children as you sing the song. Begin with one child drawing out a handful of ants. Together, count the number of ants and pass the basket as you sing the verse for that number. The child holding the basket at the end of the verse gets to draw the ants for the next verse. Count the ants as a group, sing that number's verse as the basket is passed and so on.

To Extend This Circle Time

Locate an ant farm for your science center. Count the ants in the farm.

8

TLC10064 Copyright © Teaching & Learning Company, Carthage, IL 62321

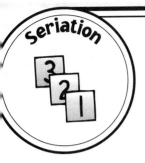

Seriation

Props/Visual Aids

Have the children make ant headbands. You can use strips of black or brown construction paper and/or pipe cleaners to have the children create their own, or use the pattern on page 10.

Talk About

Invite the children to wear their headbands as they act out the song. Begin with the children marching in single file. As the numbers increase in the song, the children march in pairs, threes and so on. Ask if any child would like to march alone and be "the little one" who stops for lots of reasons.

To Extend This Circle Time

Have the children create new words and actions for the song. Ask, "What could a group of four ants do? Seven ants?" You might have skipping, skating and sleeping ants!

Books to Share

Demuth, Patricia Brennan. *Those Amazing Ants.* Macmillan Publishing Company, 1994.
  Detailed illustrations and text describe how ants live, what they eat and some fascinating facts—such as ants nap, yawn and stretch!

Freschet, Berniece. *The Ants Go Marching.* Charles Scribner's Sons, 1973.
  Earth-tone woodcuts illustrate the ants' journey, one by one, two by two, over a leaf, under a fence, and on, always with the little ant behind.

Pinczes, Elinor J. *A Remainder of One.* Houghton Mifflin Company, 1995.
  When the queen of the bugs demands that her army march in even lines, Private Joe divides the marchers so that he will not be left out of the parade.

Van Allsburg, Chris. *Two Bad Ants.* Houghton Mifflin Company, 1988.
  Two ants desert their colony to explore a house and experience many dangerous adventures in a kitchen, before they return to their home and safety.

Wolkstein, Diane. *Step by Step.* Morrow Junior Books, 1994.
  One step at a time, a little ant journeys to visit her friend and they enjoy a day of adventure together.

Tapes and CDs

Beall, Pamela Conn, and Susan Hagen Nipp. "The Ants Go Marching" from *Wee Sing Silly Songs.* Price Stern Sloan, 1986.

Scruggs, Joe. "The Parade" from *Ants.* Educational Graphics Press, 1994.

Sharon, Lois and Bram. "The Ants Go Marching" from *Singing 'n' Swinging.* Elephant Records, 1980.

Strausman, Paul. "The Ants Go Marching" from *Camels, Cats and Rainbows.* A Gentle Wind, Inc., 1982.

10

TLC10064 Copyright © Teaching & Learning Company, Carthage, IL 62321

Apples and Bananas

I like to eat, eat, eat apples and bananas,
I like to eat, eat, eat apples and bananas,
*(Sing additional verses using the vowel sounds "A," "E," "I," "O," "U,"
to change the words **eat, apples** and **bananas**.)*

Compare/Classify

Props/Visual Aids

Provide a variety of types of apples and bananas. Give each child one, or if your group is large, divide the children into groups of two or three. You can also use the patterns on pages 14 and 15; color the fruit in a variety of realistic ways.

Talk About

Vary the words to the song by singing about the different characteristics of the apples and bananas you have supplied. You might sing, "We have some red, red, red apples in our circle." Help the children to describe the fruit by color, texture, temperature, smell and taste. Ask, "Which banana is the most green? Which is yellow? Which apples taste sour?"

To Extend This Circle Time

Locate a food dehydrator to dry slices of apples and bananas. If this isn't possible, purchase banana and apple chips from a grocery or health food store. Compare slices of fresh fruit with the dried fruit, by touching, smelling and tasting. Ask, "Which do you like best?"

TLC10064 Copyright © Teaching & Learning Company, Carthage, IL 62321

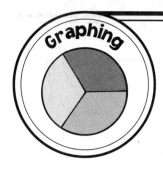

Props/Visual Aids

Supply a variety of apples and bananas or other fruit. On tagboard, make a chart with two sections. Draw a happy face on one side and a sad face on the other. Add horizontal lines according to how many types of fruit you will taste and record. On the far left, draw a simple representation of a fruit for each of the horizontal lines.

Talk About

Vary the words to the song by singing, "Who likes the red, red, red apples on the plate?" Give each child a taste of the fruit and record his or her name in the happy or sad face section of the chart according to the child's response. After every child has had a taste, count how many children are in each section.

☺

Ken	Jill	Amy	
Julie	Joe	Sue	
Eduardo	Juan	Emily	Janish
Masud	Annie		
Sue	Tomas		
Mario			

☹

Mario			
Eduardo	Ken		
Jill	Janish		
Amy	Mario		
Joe	Amy	Emily	Eduardo
Janish			

To Extend This Circle Time

You can extend this activity by graphing the class's likes and dislikes of other foods containing apples or bananas. You might try the fruit in juice, muffins, pie, bread, cookies, sauce or dried.

Props/Visual Aids

Reproduce the apple and banana patterns on pages 14 and 15 on colored paper, or color them in a variety of hues. Copy the apple and banana outlines on page 15, one page for each child. Supply the children with washable markers or crayons in the same colors as the apple and banana patterns.

Talk About

Make a simple pattern with four colored apples. Invite the children to copy the pattern by coloring the apple outlines on their pages. Ask a child to create the next pattern and help the children to duplicate it. Repeat with the banana patterns and outlines. Have the children take turns creating and copying apple and banana patterns.

To Extend This Circle Time

Provide the children with paper plates and homemade modeling dough (or a commercial product) in red, yellow and green. Encourage the children to form the dough into apples and bananas and arrange their fruit into patterns on the paper plates.

TLC10064 Copyright © Teaching & Learning Company, Carthage, IL 62321

Sorting

Props/Visual Aids

Provide a variety of apples and bananas for the children to sort, or use the patterns on pages 14 and 15 in a variety of colors.

Talk About

Vary the words to the song to give the children direction in sorting the fruit. You might sing, "Where is the red, red, red fruit for the pile?" or "Put the long, long, long bananas all together." Ask the children to sort the fruit by color: the red, green and yellow in separate piles. For younger children, you may wish to use only one type of fruit at a time. With older children, use both apples and bananas as well as other types of fruit. Ask, "Can an apple and a banana both be in the yellow group? The green group?"

To Extend This Circle Time

Have the children make fruit salad. Plastic knives work well for cutting most fruit and are fairly safe for children to use with close supervision. Mix all the cut-up fruit together in a large bowl and serve for snack. Place each child's portion on a large paper plate, and ask him or her to sort the different types of fruit on the plate. Invite the children to eat the groups of apples, bananas and grapes separately, or mix them all together again and enjoy!

Books to Share

Charles, N.N. *What Am I? Looking Through Shapes at Apples and Grapes.* Blue Sky Press, 1994.
 Big, bright illustrations with cut-out shapes and rhyming questions introduce fruits, colors and shapes.

Ehlert, Lois. *Eating the Alphabet.* Harcourt Brace Jovanovich, 1989.
 A brightly illustrated alphabetical tour of the world of fruits and vegetables, from apricot and artichoke to yam and zucchini.

Maestro, Betsy. *How Do Apples Grow?* HarperCollins, 1992.
 Simple text and detailed illustrations describe the life cycle of an apple, from a spring bud to flower to fruit.

McMillan, Bruce. *Growing Colors.* Lothrop, Lee & Shepard Books, 1988.
 Photographs of green peas, red raspberries, purple plums and other fruits and vegetables illustrate the many colors of nature.

Tryon, Leslie. *Albert's Field Trip.* Atheneum, 1993.
 Albert leads a class on a memorable field trip to an apple farm, where they pick apples, watch apples being squeezed into juice and eat apple pies.

Tapes and CDs

Fisher, Cilla, and Artie Trezise. "Apples and Bananas" from *The Singing Kettle: Scots Sing-Along Songs for Children.* Kettle Records, 1982.

Pease, Tom. "Apples and Bananas" from *Boogie, Boogie, Boogie.* Tomorrow River Music, 1985.

Raffi. "Apples and Bananas" from *One Light, One Sun.* Troubadour Records, 1985.

Rappin' Rob. "Lima Beans and Diced Beets" from *The Rappin' Rob Rap.* The Kid-Tested Company, 1992.

TLC10064 Copyright © Teaching & Learning Company, Carthage, IL 62321

14

TLC10064 Copyright © Teaching & Learning Company, Carthage, IL 62321

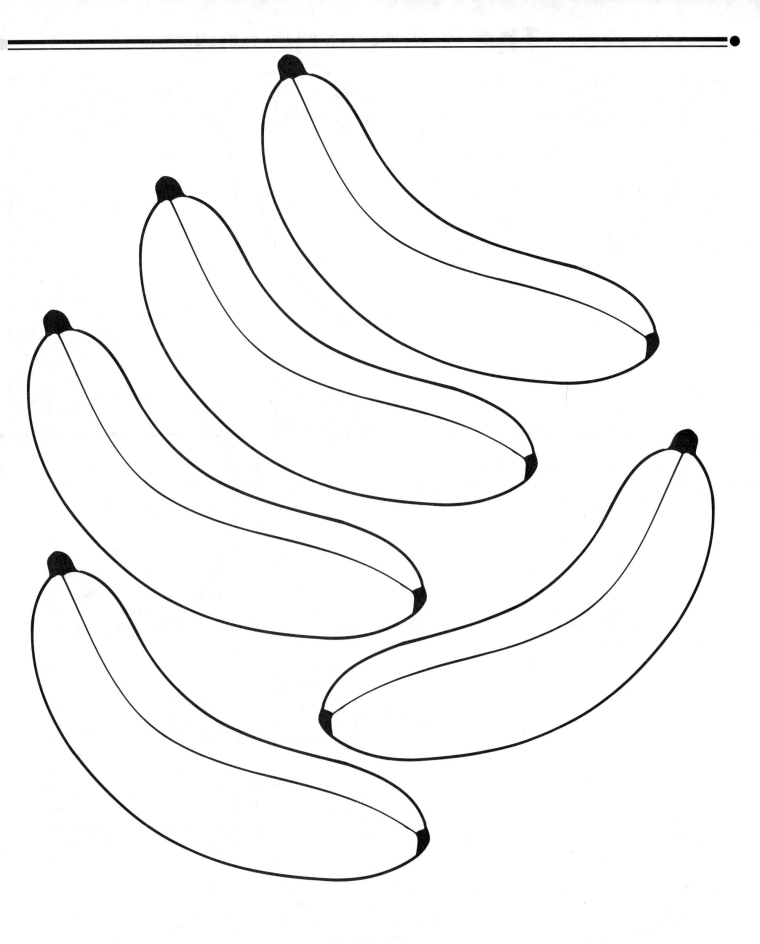

TLC10064 Copyright © Teaching & Learning Company, Carthage, IL 62321

The Barnyard Song

I had a bird and the bird pleased me,
I fed my bird on yonder tree.
Bird goes fid-dle-ee-fee.

I had a hen and the hen pleased me,
I fed my hen on yonder tree.
Hen goes chim-my-chuck, chim-my-chuck.
Bird goes fid-dle-ee-fee.
(Verses: Add animals and repeat previous animals and sounds.)
Duck: goes quack, quack, quack, quack.
Goose: goes swishy, swishy.
Sheep: goes baa-baa, baa-baa.
Pig: goes oink, oink, oink, oink.
Cow: goes moo, moo, moo, moo.
Horse: goes neigh, neigh, neigh, neigh.

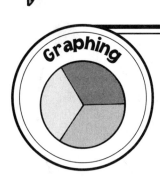

Props/Visual Aids
Find plastic models of the animals in the song. On chart paper make a graph with a section for each type of animal. Title the graph "The Animals on Our Farm."

Talk About
Sing the song and and ask the children which of the animals they would like to have on their farm. Give each child a plastic animal of the kind they chose. If you cannot find enough plastic animals, use the patterns on pages 20 and 21. Ask them to place their animals under the corresponding section of the graph. Count the number of animals in each section and mark that number on the graph.

To Extend This Circle Time
Create a farm in your dramatic play area. Provide stuffed animals, toy farm machinery, shovels, hats and boots. Bring in a bale of hay. Attach a large piece of paper to the wall and draw a farm mural.

The Animals on Our Farm							
Cow	Bird	Pig	Duck	Hen	Horse	Sheep	Goose
					🐴	🐑	
		🐷			🐴	🐑	
🐄		🐷	🦆		🐴	🐑	
🐄		🐷	🦆	🐔	🐴	🐑	
🐄	🐦	🐷	🦆	🐔	🐴	🐑	🐔
🐄	🐦	🐷	🦆	🐔	🐴	🐑	🐔
4	2	5	4	3	6	6	2

TLC10064 Copyright © Teaching & Learning Company, Carthage, IL 62321

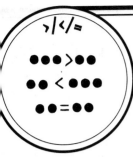

Props/Visual Aids

Reproduce the tree pattern on page 19. Make several copies of the animal patterns on pages 20 and 21. Color and prepare the patterns for use on the flannel board.

Talk About

Place the tree in the center of the flannel board. Invite the children to take turns putting different combinations of animals under the tree. Count each set of animals. Ask, "How many ducks are under the tree? How many pigs? Are there more pigs or more ducks?"

To Extend This Circle Time

Mix several kinds of dry cereal together to make an "animal feed" snack. You might use O-shaped, square and round cereals. Give each child a paper plate and small scoop of the cereal mix. Ask, "How many O-shapes did you get? Do you have more squares or more round shapes?" Be sure to ask what kind of animal each child is, as he or she enjoys the snack.

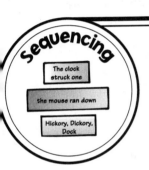

Props/Visual Aids

Reproduce, color and laminate the patterns on pages 20 and 21.

Talk About

Give an animal to each child. You may want to make duplicates of the animals so each child has one to hold. As you sing the song, have the children hold up the animal for that verse. If you have younger children, you may want to arrange them (and their animals) in the same sequence as the song. Then try singing the song's verses in a different sequence.

To Extend This Circle Time

Have the children make paper bag puppets of the animals in the song. Supply the art center with lunch-size paper bags, construction paper scraps, yarn, safety scissors, glue and washable markers. You may wish to precut eyes, ears, mouths and noses for the various animals.

TLC10064 Copyright © Teaching & Learning Company, Carthage, IL 62321

Sorting

Props/Visual Aids

Use the animal patterns on pages 20 and 21 to make multiple copies. Color them in a variety of ways. You might make all of one kind of animal the same color (all blue pigs) or make one animal many colors.

Talk About

Vary the words to the song to help the children sort the animals. You might sing, "Jim has the pigs, the pigs have Jim, give your pigs to Jim right now" or "Kasey has red geese, red geese are Kasey's, give your red geese to Kasey right now."

To Extend This Circle Time

Take a field trip to a real farm or petting zoo that has farm animals. Before you go, talk about the animals you will see. Have the children record their trip by drawing pictures of the animals to make a class book.

Books to Share

Brown, Craig. *My Barn*. Greenwillow Books, 1991.
   The farmer visits and feeds each of the animals in the barn and listens to the sounds they make.

Carroll, Kathleen Sullivan. *One Red Rooster*. Houghton Mifflin Company, 1992.
   The numbers one through ten are introduced in rhymed text and bright illustrations of a variety of rather noisy farm animals.

Cazet, Denys. *Nothing at All*. Orchard Books, 1994.
   As the farm animals awake, each has something to say, except the scarecrow who says nothing at all, until he discovers the mouse in his pants.

Fleming, Denise. *Barnyard Banter*. Henry Holt and Company, 1994.
   Handmade paper illustrations full of texture and color illustrate a noisy morning on the farm, with clucking and mucking, cooing and mewing.

Lillie, Patricia. *When the Rooster Crowed*. Greenwillow Books, 1991.
   Not until all the animals join voices is the farmer able to get out of bed in the morning and feed them.

McPhail, David. *Farm Morning*. Harcourt Brace Jovanovich, 1985.
   A father and his young daughter share a special morning as they feed all the animals on their farm.

Tresselt, Alvin. *Wake Up, Farm!* Lothrop, Lee & Shepard Books, 1991.
   Realistic watercolors and simple descriptive text evoke the sounds and sights of a country morning on a family farm.

Zimmerman, Andrea. *The Cow Buzzed*. HarperCollins Publishers, 1993.
   When the farm animals give one another a cold, they pass along their distinctive voices along with the coughs, sniffles and sneezes.

Tapes and CDs

Fisher, Cilla, and Artie Trezise. "I Had a Hen" from *The Singing Kettle 2: Scots Sing-Along Songs for Kids*. Kettle Records, 1984.

Glazer, Tom. "Barnyard Song" from *Let's Sing Fingerplays*. CMS Records, Inc., 1977.

Roth, Kevin. "The Barnyard Song" from *Animal Crackers and Other Tasty Tunes*. CMS Records, Inc., 1988.

18

TLC10064 Copyright © Teaching & Learning Company, Carthage, IL 62321

20

TLC10064 Copyright © Teaching & Learning Company, Carthage, IL 62321

TLC10064 Copyright © Teaching & Learning Company, Carthage, IL 62321

Five Green and Speckled Frogs

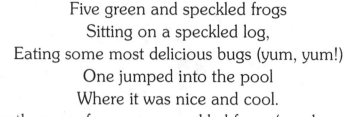

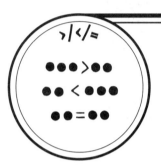

Five green and speckled frogs
Sitting on a speckled log,
Eating some most delicious bugs (yum, yum!)
One jumped into the pool
Where it was nice and cool.
Now there are four green speckled frogs (croak, croak!)
(Repeat, counting down frogs to "no green speckled frogs.")

Props/Visual Aids

Using the patterns on pages 25 and 26, make two logs and 10 frogs. Color and laminate for durability.

Talk About

Place both logs on the flannel board. Ask the children to help you count out five frogs and place them on one of the logs. Count out three frogs and place them on the other log. Ask, "Which log has more frogs? Which log has fewer frogs?" Repeat, using different combinations of frogs.

To Extend This Circle Time

Make "bugs on a log" for a snack. Give each child a piece of celery and a small portion of peanut butter or cream cheese to use as filling. The children can use plastic knives or large craft sticks to spread the filling on their celery. Give each child a small amount of raisins or chocolate chips. Ask them to count out the raisins or chips and place on their "log." Ask, "Which log has the most? Which log has the fewest?" Enjoy your snack!

TLC10064 Copyright © Teaching & Learning Company, Carthage, IL 62321

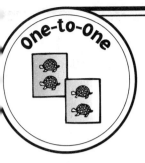

One-to-One

Props/Visual Aids

Reproduce and color the frog patterns on page 25 or 27 and laminate. You will need a wipe-off marker to write numerals on the frogs. Provide a small cup of raisins and a tissue for each child.

Talk About

Give each child a frog and sing the song. Ask each child how many bugs his or her frog should eat and write that numeral on the frog. For younger children, write the numeral and add the corresponding number of dots. Ask the children to count out that number of raisins on their tissues. Have the children pretend to be the frogs as they eat their raisins; it's great fun!

To Extend This Circle Time

Use your circle time rug as the frogs' cool pool, or use masking tape on the floor for a pool outline. Have the children gather at the edge of the pool. Sing the song again using the number of children in the group for the first verse. (If your group is large, divide it into two groups on either side of the pool.) Have the children act out the song, one jumping into the pool for each verse and then counting how many frogs would start the next verse. Ask, "What are the frogs in the pool doing? What do *you* do at the pool?"

Patterning

Props/Visual Aids

Collect a variety of frog items. You might find stickers, gift wrap, greeting cards, stuffed frogs and plastic frogs. Choose several simple and related categories (colors or size or what the frogs are made from), and ask the children to help you sort the frogs into piles. You might choose plastic frogs, paper frogs and fuzzy frogs.

Talk About

Start a simple pattern in the center of the circle. You might have two paper frogs, one plastic frog, two paper frogs. Ask, "What kind of frog do we need next?" Ask a child to choose a frog from the correct pile and add it to the pattern. You can repeat the exercise, making the pattern more difficult or adding a third type of frog.

To Extend This Circle Time

Use the frog items you have collected to make a frog center. Place the plastic and stuffed frogs and books about frogs (see "Books to Share") on a small table under a bulletin board display of the paper frogs. Make copies of the frog patterns on page 25 or 27. Have the children color the frogs with crayons, watercolors or washable markers. Ask the children to help create a pattern when you use their frogs as a border for the bulletin board.

Sorting

Props/Visual Aids
Make several copies of the frog patterns on page 25 or 27 and cut out. Reproduce the log pattern on page 26 to make three logs.

Talk About
Ask the children to sort the frogs by shape or sitting position so the identical frogs are grouped together. Place the logs on the circle time rug and mix the frogs again. Invite the children to take turns choosing a frog to put on a log, sorting the frogs so that only identical frogs share the same log.

To Extend This Circle Time
Find pictures of a variety of frogs. Nature magazines such as *Ranger Rick* and *Your Big Backyard* are excellent sources. Laminate the pictures for durability. Ask the children to sort the frogs in a variety of ways first by color, size, type of frog and so on.

Books to Share
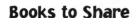

Arnold, Tedd. *Green Wilma*. Dial Books for Young Readers, 1993.
   Humorous illustrations and a rhyming text tell the story of Wilma, who wakes up green and disrupts home and school as she searches for tasty flies.

Fowler, Allan. *Frogs and Toads and Tadpoles, Too*. Childrens Press, Inc., 1992.
   Clear photographs and very simple text explain basic likenesses and differences between frogs and toads.

Kalan, Robert. *Jump, Frog, Jump!* Mulberrry Books, 1981.
   Colorful illustrations depict the action in this cumulative tale about a frog who tries to catch a fly without getting caught itself!

Manushkin, Fran. *Peeping and Sleeping*. Clarion Books, 1994.
   Barry and his father take an evening walk to investigate the strange peeping sounds they hear and find a surprise down at the pond.

Pfeffer, Wendy. *From Tadpole to Frog*. HarperCollins, 1994.
   Detailed drawings and simple text describe the first two years of a frog's life and its metamorphosis from tadpole to frog.

Taylor, Kim. *Frog*. Dutton Children's Books, 1991.
   Clear photographs and simple text show the development of a frog from egg through the first year.

Wing, Natasha. *Hippity Hop, Frog on Top*. Simon & Schuster, 1994.
   Bright, bold paintings illustrate 10 curious frogs as one by one they pile up, trying to see what's on the other side of a wall.

Tapes and CDs

Friedl, Denise. "Five Little Speckled Frogs" from *Tickle-a-Toe*. Castle Capers Music, 1992.

Jackson, Mike and Michelle. "Five Little Speckled Frogs" from *Playmates*. Elephant Records, 1983.

Monet, Lisa. "Five Little Speckled Frogs" from *Circle Time: Songs and Rhymes for the Very Young*. Monet Productions, 1986.

Raffi. "Five Little Frogs" from *The Singable Songs Collection*. Shoreline/A&M Records, 1988.

Raffi with Ken Whiteley. "Five Little Frogs" from *Singable Songs for the Very Young*. Shoreline, 1979.

TLC10064 Copyright © Teaching & Learning Company, Carthage, IL 62321

TLC10064 Copyright © Teaching & Learning Company, Carthage, IL 62321

TLC10064 Copyright © Teaching & Learning Company, Carthage, IL 62321

Five Little Chickadees

Five little chickadees sitting on a door,
One flew away and then there were four.
(chorus)
Chickadee, chickadee, happy and gay,
Chickadee, chickadee, fly, fly away.
(verses)
Four little chickadees sitting in a tree,
One flew away and then there were three.
Three little chickadees sitting on a shoe,
One flew away and then there were two.
Two little chickadees sitting by a bun,
One flew away and then there was one.
One little chickadee sitting all alone,
It flew away and then there were none.
Five little chickadees flying far away,
Come back, chickadees, it's time to play.

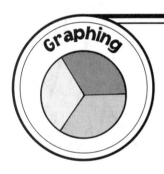

Graphing

Props/Visual Aids

Using your library as a resource, determine which birds are commonly seen in your area at the time of this lesson. Bird-watching handbooks or field guides will also show detailed illustrations of the birds for identification. Using poster board, make a bird-watching graph. Depending on the skill level of your group, you may choose to graph just the number of birds observed each day or to graph specific types of birds. Make copies of the generic bird outline on page 31 and tape them to the graph to record the number of birds observed.

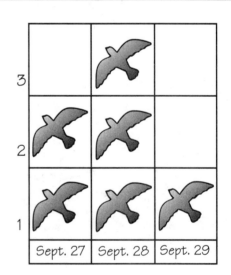

Talk About

Place the bird-watching graph, pictures of birds and other resource materials and binoculars near a classroom window. Set aside specified times throughout the day for groups of children to observe birds. Discuss which and how many birds each group saw and place the bird cut-outs on the corresponding columns of the graph.

To Extend This Circle Time

Take a field trip to a local aviary or nature preserve. Count and graph the number and/or kinds of birds you see.

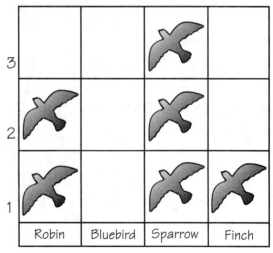

TLC10064 Copyright © Teaching & Learning Company, Carthage, IL 62321

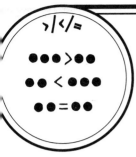

Props/Visual Aids

Purchase bird stickers or a rubber stamp showing a bird. Place varying amounts (from one to five or more depending on the skill level of your children) of stickers or stamped images on index cards, one card for each child.

Talk About

Give each child one of the cards. Together, count the number of birds each child has. Ask, "Who has the most birds? How many more birds does Jimmy need to have as many as Lisa?" Go around the group, counting and adding stickers or stamps until all the cards have an equal number.

To Extend This Circle Time

Make bird mobiles to decorate your classroom. Reproduce on sturdy paper the patterns on page 31. Have the children cut out the body and wing shapes, and assist them in cutting the slit for the wings. Supply the children with washable markers or paint, glue and craft feathers to decorate their birds. Hang the birds from the ceiling using paper clips and fishing line.

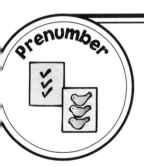

Props/Visual Aids

Reproduce the chickadee patterns on page 32. Make enough so that each child has one set of five chickadees. Color and laminate for durability.

Talk About

Give each child five chickadees and count them out together. As you sing the song, have the children remove one of their chickadees for each verse. Count the remaining birds after each verse. Next, have the children sit in groups of five and pretend to be the chickadees. As you sing the song, have one child "fly away" for each verse.

To Extend This Circle Time

Go for a bird walk and count the birds that you see. Purchase a bird feeder or make bird treats with your class. Spread peanut butter on pinecones and roll in birdseed. Use yarn or pipe cleaners to hang the pinecones in nearby trees, outside your classroom window or near your playground. Watch the bird feeders and list the birds you see. Provide bird books to help the children identify the birds they observe.

Relationships

Props/Visual Aids

Bring in several of the wonderful books on different kinds of birds and allow the children to look through them. You may also enlarge the illustrations on pages 33 and 34 and color appropriately. You will need chart paper and markers.

Talk About

Encourage the children to discuss the characteristics of the different types of birds, how they are alike or different. Ask, "What is something that every bird has?" List the children's responses on the chart paper, with a number and a simple drawing of the characteristic. You might have "two wings, feathers, a beak, two feet."

To Extend This Circle Time

Have your children build their own bird nests. You might use several cupcake liners or plastic berry baskets for a base. Dried grass, small sticks, excelsior packing material, colored "Easter grass," modeling clay and papier-mâché can all be used for building materials. Display the nests in a bird center in your science area. Encourage the children to bring in feathers and try to identify them using the bird books you have selected. Borrow a caged pet bird for a day's visit. How is that bird like the birds observed outside the classroom?

Books to Share

Ehlert, Lois. *Feathers for Lunch.* Harcourt Brace Jovanovich, 1990.
 Colorful illustrations and rhyming text introduce a hungry house cat and 12 common birds he tries unsuccessfully to catch for lunch.

Rockwell, Anne. *Our Yard Is Full of Birds.* Macmillan, 1992.
 Accurate paintings help tell the story of a little boy and the birds he likes to watch through all the seasons of the year, including swallows, mourning doves, chickadees and jays.

Royston, Angela. *Birds.* Alladin Books, 1992.
 Brief text and clear photographs describe the sparrow, duck, eagle, parrot, hummingbird and more.

Sill, Cathryn. *About Birds: A Guide for Children.* Peachtree Publishers, 1991.
 Very simple text and detailed illustrations introduce the world of birds from eggs to flight, from songs to nests.

Wolff, Ashley. *A Year of Birds.* Dodd, Mead & Company, 1984.
 Brightly colored linoleum block prints and simple text introduce the birds that visit Ellie's house during the changing seasons.

Tapes and CDs

Blackburn, Sally, and David White. "Five Little Chickadees" from *Singing Games.* Tom Thumb Records, 1982.

Monet, Lisa. "Chickadee" from *My Best Friend.* Music for Little People, 1991.

Sharon, Lois and Bram. "Five Little Chickadees" from *Mainly Mother Goose: Songs and Rhymes for Merry Young Souls.* Elephant Records, 1984.

TLC10064 Copyright © Teaching & Learning Company, Carthage, IL 62321

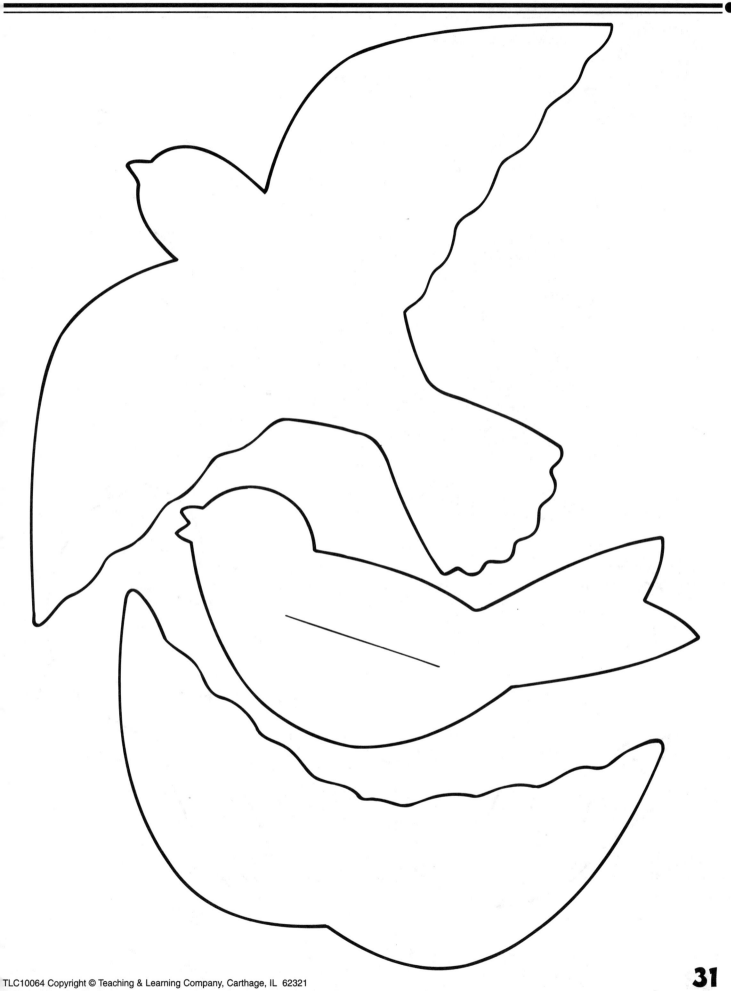

TLC10064 Copyright © Teaching & Learning Company, Carthage, IL 62321

TLC10064 Copyright © Teaching & Learning Company, Carthage, IL 62321

TLC10064 Copyright © Teaching & Learning Company, Carthage, IL 62321

34

TLC10064 Copyright © Teaching & Learning Company, Carthage, IL 62321

Five Little Ducks

Five little ducks went out to play,
Over the hills and far away.
Mama duck said, "Quack, quack, quack, quack."
But only four little ducks came back.
(Additional verses count backwards)
Four little ducks . . . only three little ducks came back
Three little ducks . . . only two little ducks came back
Two little ducks . . . only one little duck came back
One little duck . . . no little ducks came back.
No little ducks . . . five little ducks came running back.

(You may want to try these actions to the song, or make up your own.)
Line 1: Hold up fingers to represent ducks.
Line 2: Move arm as if going over hills, look far away with hand shading eyes.
Line 3: Hold both hands to make quacking motion.
Line 4: Hold up fingers to represent ducks.

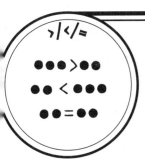

Props/Visual Aids
Use the duck pattern on page 38 to make five ducks for each child. A piece of yarn or tape on the floor can divide each child's space for the ducks to "go out to play" and "come back."

Talk About
As you sing the song, have the children move their ducks with the words. Stop at the end of each verse. Ask, "How many ducks are over the hills and far away? How many came back? Where are there more ducks? Where are there fewer ducks?" Allow plenty of time for the children to manipulate and count their ducks.

To Extend This Circle Time
Divide the children into groups of six. Ask who in each group would like to be the mother or father duck. Designate an area in the classroom to be "over the hills and far away" and have the children act out the song as you sing the words. You might want to assign numbers to the children (give each child a duck with a numeral 1 to 5 written on it) to provide cues for staying or coming back. If the verse is "four little ducks came back," ducks four, three, two and one would return to the mother or father duck.

TLC10064 Copyright © Teaching & Learning Company, Carthage, IL 62321

Props/Visual Aids

Use the pattern on page 38 to make ducks in a variety of colors or purchase duck cut-outs in colored paper or felt. A small piece of rolled tape will attach paper ducks to a flannel board.

Talk About

Place five ducks on the flannel board. As you sing the song, add a color to each verse. You might sing, "Five little ducks went out to play . . . Mama duck asked red duck to come home. Red duck said, 'Bye' and came right along." Create a simple color pattern with the five ducks. Ask, "What color would we need now to add to the pattern?" Add several more ducks and then begin the song again, to create another pattern with five ducks.

To Extend This Circle Time

Supply the children with crayons or washable markers and a copy of the duck outline patterns on page 38. Create a simple pattern of five ducks on the flannel board and ask the children to color their pages to match.

Props/Visual Aids

Use the duck pattern on page 38 to create several sets of ducks. Write the numerals 1 to 5 on a set of the ducks or a sequential phrase such as "ABCDE." You might also write the letters of the children's names (changing the number of ducks in the song to match the number of letters in a child's name).

Talk About

Place a set of ducks in sequential order on the flannel board. As you sing the song together, remove the ducks. When all of the ducks come back, ask the children to help you put them back in the correct sequence.

To Extend This Circle Time

Make a file folder game. Use the pattern on page 38 to create several sets of paper ducks. Use a different color for each set. Label the ducks with sequential numbers, letters or patterns (quarter circle, half circle, three-quarters circle, full circle). Ask the children to arrange the ducks in sequence. Give each child enough ducks to write each letter of the child's name. Have the children practice putting their own names in sequence; then ask them to work with a friend on his or her name.

TLC10064 Copyright © Teaching & Learning Company, Carthage, IL 62321

Seriation

Props/Visual Aids

Use a copy machine to reduce and enlarge the duck pattern on page 38. Plan the number of ducks and percentage of size change from one duck to the next according to the skill level of your class. Laminate the ducks and use pieces of rolled tape to adhere them to the flannel board.

Talk About

Place the ducks in random order on the flannel board. Have the children help you arrange them from smallest duck to largest. Mix the ducks and repeat the activity, placing the ducks largest to smallest.

To Extend This Circle Time

Invite the children to bring any rubber or plush ducks they may have at home. Be sure to label the ducks since many of the bath toys will be similar. Sit in a circle, each child holding a duck. Decide together which duck is the smallest and working as a group, line up a duck parade from the smallest duck to largest.

Books to Share

Beck, Ian. *Five Little Ducks*. Henry Holt and Company, 1992.
Bright illustrations depict the adventures of the five little ducks as they encounter a fox in this traditional counting rhyme.

Gerstein, Mordicai. *Follow Me!* William Morrow and Company, 1983.
A flock of hungry ducks and two geese, each bird a different color, become completely lost while trying to find their way home for dinner.

Miles, Miska. *Swim Little Duck*. Little, Brown and Company, 1976.
Little Duck ventures out to see the world but eventually decides that her pond is the best place to be.

Raffi. *Five Little Ducks*. Crown, 1989.
From the series Raffi Songs to Read. When her five little ducks disappear one by one, Mother Duck sets out to find them.

Stehr, Frédéric. *Quack-Quack*. Farrar, Straus and Giroux, 1987.
Softly colored illustrations and simple text tell the story of Quack-Quack's search for his mother.

Tafuri, Nancy. *Have You Seen My Duckling?* Puffin Books, 1986.
In detailed drawings, the reader helps the mother duck and the rest of her brood search for one missing duckling.

Wellington, Monica. *All My Little Ducklings*. E.P. Dutton, 1989.
Bright, collage-like pictures and very simple text tell the story of seven ducklings' adventures in their pond, through a barnyard and orchard and finally home to their nest.

Tapes and CDs

Buchman, Rachel. "Five Little Ducks" from *Hello Everybody*. A Gentle Wind, 1986.

McGrath, Bob, and Katharine Smithrim. "Five Little Ducks" from *Songs & Games for Toddlers*. Kids' Records, 1985.

Monet, Lisa. "Four Little Ducks" from *Circle Time: Songs and Rhymes for the Very Young*. Monet Productions, 1986.

Raffi. "Five Little Ducks" from *Raffi in Concert with the Rise and Shine Band*. Troubadour Records, 1989.

Raffi with Ken Whiteley. "Five Little Ducks" from *Rise and Shine*. Shoreline, 1982.

38

TLC10064 Copyright © Teaching & Learning Company, Carthage, IL 62321

Hickety, Pickety, My Black Hen

Hickety, pickety, my black hen,
She lays eggs for gentlemen.
Sometimes nine and sometimes ten,
Hickety, pickety, my black hen.

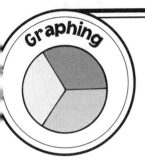

Graphing

Props/Visual Aids

Reproduce the egg pattern on page 43 and write each child's name on an egg. On chart paper, create a picture graph showing different ways eggs can be prepared. Use pictures from magazines, make simple sketches or use the patterns on page 42. You might find scrambled, hard-boiled, fried or poached eggs for your graph.

We Like Eggs!

🥚	Susie	Mario			
🥣	Kyle	Jon	Katie		
🥪	Rosa				
🍳	Min	Molly			
🍳	Juan				

Talk About

Discuss the many ways to prepare eggs. Ask, "Which kind of egg is your favorite?" You may wish to cook some eggs and conduct a taste test! After deliberations, have the children place their egg pattern in the section of the graph showing their favorite egg dish. Ask, "Which kind of egg do the most children like?" One note of caution: since eggs are a common allergen, you may wish to inform parents before doing this activity or the one following.

To Extend This Circle Time

Make egg salad with your class. You will need a hand-operated grinder, several bowls, mixing spoons, mayonnaise, mustard, salt and boiled eggs. Have the children wash their hands and begin peeling the eggs. When all the shell is removed, assist each child in grinding his or her egg into a large bowl. Add mayonnaise, a small amount of mustard and a dash of salt. Spread the egg salad on crackers and enjoy your snack!

TLC10064 Copyright © Teaching & Learning Company, Carthage, IL 62321

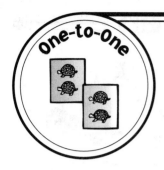

Props/Visual Aids
Collect small plastic eggs, such as the inexpensive kind available at Easter, or use the large egg pattern on page 42 to make 20 eggs.

Talk About
Use the eggs for a counting game. Vary the words to the song by singing a child's name and choosing different numbers of eggs. You might sing, "She lays eggs for Justin, sometimes two and sometimes four." Justin can then count out two eggs in a row and then another row of four eggs. Compare the two groups of eggs by arranging them side by side. The numbers you choose to sing about will depend on the skill level of your group.

To Extend This Circle Time
Hard-boil enough eggs so that each child may have an egg to decorate. You may choose to use stickers, markers, crayons, glue, yarn scraps or washable paint. Be sure to have several extra eggs on hand in case any eggs are broken during the enthusiastic decorating and explain to the class the temporary nature of their creations. Small strips of paper taped to form a circle or bottle caps can serve as egg stands for a display.

Props/Visual Aids
Reproduce the hen and egg patterns on page 43. Make 10 of each, cut out and laminate for durability. You could also use 10 plastic eggs instead of the egg pattern. Write the numerals 1 to 10 on the hens.

Talk About
As you sing the song, show one of the hens to the children. Together, count out the number of eggs to match the numeral written on the hen. Repeat with other hens, inviting children to take turns counting out the number of eggs needed, as the class counts as a group.

To Extend This Circle Time
Make an egg matching game. On sturdy paper, reproduce the large egg pattern on page 42. Make 10 eggs in the same color. On one half of each egg write a numeral from 1 to 10. On the other half of the egg, place the corresponding amount of dots or small stickers. Cut each egg in half, using jagged and unique cuts, so only the correct halves will fit together. Laminate the halves for durability and place the pieces in a folder available to the children.

40

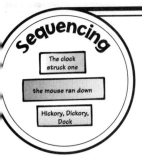

Props/Visual Aids

Find books about the life cycle of a chicken (see "Books to Share") or find other pictures showing the hatching and growth of a chick. Reproduce, color and cut out the pictures on page 44.

Talk About

Share the books about chickens with the class. Ask, "Which do you think came first, the chicken or the egg?" Show the class the pictures you have prepared. "Which picture do you think comes first? Next?" Help the children discover that the cycle will continue as the grown chicken lays a new egg. Continue to move the cards to create the next cycle.

To Extend This Circle Time

There are many books on the life cycles of other creatures that hatch from eggs. Share Jane Burton's *Chick* with your class. As a group, act out the sequence of egg to hatching to growing animal. Have the children take turns suggesting what animal to dramatize, or invite a group of children to act out the animal and the remaining children guess which animal's cycle they are portraying.

Books to Share

Burton, Jane. *Chick*. Lodestar Books, 1992.
Clear photographs and simple text show the development of a chick from the egg stage to the eighth week.

Hariton, Anca. *Egg Story*. Dutton Children's Books, 1992.
From a white spot on a yolk to a wet and weary chick that has struggled out of its shell, each stage of growth inside the egg is simply and accurately presented in text and pictures.

Lane, Megan Halsey. *Something to Crow About*. Dial Books for Young Readers, 1990.
Two chicks who look just the same find out how different they are when one starts to lay eggs and the other starts to crow.

McGovern, Ann. *Eggs on Your Nose*. Macmillan, 1987.
Humorous illustrations and rhyming text relate the utter mess made by a child eating eggs.

Wormell, Mary. *Hilda Hen's Search*. Harcourt Brace & Company, 1994.
Hilda tries several places before she finds the right spot to lay and hatch her eggs.

Tapes and CDs

Rashad, Phylicia. "My Black Hen" from *Baby's Nursery Rhymes*. Lightyear Records, 1991.

TLC10064 Copyright © Teaching & Learning Company, Carthage, IL 62321

TLC10064 Copyright © Teaching & Learning Company, Carthage, IL 62321

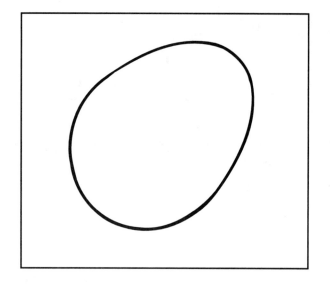

44

TLC10064 Copyright © Teaching & Learning Company, Carthage, IL 62321

Hickory, Dickory, Dock

Hickory, dickory, dock
The mouse ran up the clock.
The clock struck one,
The mouse ran down,
Hickory, dickory, dock.

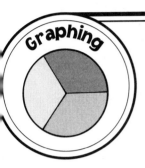

Graphing

Props/Visual Aids

You will need large chart paper and markers. Depending on the age and skill level of your group of children, you may want to provide pictures or real items of the things you choose to graph.

Talk About

There are many graphing activities you can do with clocks. Graph the types of clocks the children have in their homes. Ask, "What kind of clock do you have in your kitchen? Bedroom? Living room?" You could also graph times of day, such as a child's favorite time of day at school, at home or what time a favorite TV show is on.

My Favorite Time of Day

| 7:00 Wake Up | 9:30 Snack | 10:00 Story | 12:00 Lunch | 5:00 Go Home | 8:00 Bedtime |

To Extend This Circle Time

Set up a clock store in your dramatic play area. Ask parents to bring clocks from home or visit thrift stores to purchase a variety of clocks. Display the clocks on shelves and invite the children to set them for different times. Find old clocks for the children to take apart. They will love using small tools, and the inner workings of a clock are fascinating!

TLC10064 Copyright © Teaching & Learning Company, Carthage, IL 62321

Props/Visual Aids

Reproduce the clock face and hands patterns on page 48 and attach only one hand with a brad. You might also use, if available, a large classroom clock with movable hands available from some classroom suppliers, a digital clock with movable numbers (not an LED model) or a large wind-up clock. Reproduce the mice patterns on page 49 or give each child 12 small plastic mice.

Talk About

Set the clock's hand for a specific time and ask the children to count out that number of plastic mice. You can vary the words of the song to change the time and the number of mice running up and down the clock. Give a child a specific number of mice (three), and then ask the child to set the clock's hand on that number (3:00).

To Extend This Circle Time

Supply each child with two black construction paper squares (approximately 5" [13 cm] square) and safety scissors. Ask them to trim each corner of the squares to make a circular shape. Glue or tape the circles to a 1¹/₂" (4 cm) wide strip of construction paper long enough to fit around a child's head to make simple mouse ear headbands. Draw a large clock face on butcher paper and place it at one end of your circle time area. Invite the children to act out the song. Change the words to continue counting. You might sing, "Three mice ran up the clock" as three children run to the top of the clock. Pause after the words: *The clock struck three* to allow the waiting mice to call out the number of strikes, "One, two, three!"

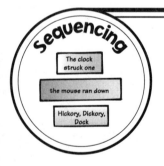
Props/Visual Aids

Reproduce the clock patterns on page 48. Laminate for durability and attach the hands with a brad at the center of the clock. Make a large chart showing the daily schedule for the class. Draw a clock face and write the corresponding time for each scheduled activity.

My Morning Routine		
⏰	7:00 a.m.	Wake up
⏰	7:10 a.m.	Get dressed
⏰	7:15 a.m.	Eat breakfast
⏰	7:35 a.m.	Leave for school

Talk About

It is important for children to understand the sequence of events and activities in your class's daily routine. "After art, we have snack, and then we go outside." Show the chart to the group and discuss the sequence. Vary the words to the song to describe the schedule. You might sing, "Hickory, dickory, dock. The class looks at the clock. The clock strikes 10, it's time for snack, hickory, dickory, dock." Move the hand of the large clock to the corresponding time.

TLC10064 Copyright © Teaching & Learning Company, Carthage, IL 62321

To Extend This Circle Time

Ask children and their parents to make a similar schedule showing a "typical" evening at home, or just the bedtime or morning routines.

Sorting

Props/Visual Aids

Reproduce the mice patterns on page 49. Use a copy machine to enlarge and reduce some of the mice. Color in a variety of colors, cut out and laminate for durability.

Talk About

Have the children sort the mice by color, shape or size. Begin by defining two categories, such as large and small or gray and brown. Give each child several mice and invite him or her to place the mice in the correct group.

To Extend This Circle Time

Borrow or consider purchasing a mouse for a classroom pet. Observe the mouse carefully. Ask, "Have any of you seen a live mouse before? Did that mouse look like this one? Was it the same color? Larger or smaller? Does this mouse look like the mice in our books? How is it different?"

Books to Share

Aylesworth, Jim. *Two Terrible Frights*. Atheneum, 1987.
A little girl mouse and a little girl person meet while getting a snack in the kitchen at bedtime and scare each other, only to dream of each other later.

Henrietta. *A Mouse in the House*. Dorling Kindersley, 1991.
The reader is invited to search for the mouse on each page of photographs showing many objects found in a house preparing for a birthday party.

Miller, Moira. *Oscar Mouse Finds a Home*. Dial Books for Young Readers, 1985.
Oscar searches for a quiet home of his own when the attic where he lives becomes too crowded with little brothers and sisters.

Noll, Sally. *Watch Where You Go*. Greenwillow Books, 1990.
A gray mouse runs through what appears to be grass, rocks and tree branches to a safe and happy ending.

Watts, Barrie. *Mouse*. Lodestar Books, See How They Grow Series, 1992.
Clear photographs and simple text show the development of a mouse from birth to eight weeks old.

Tapes and CDs

Barolk Folk with Madeline MacNeil and Barbara Hess. "Hickory Dickory Dock" from *Girls and Boys, Come Out to Play*. Music for Little People, 1991.

Beall, Pamela Conn, and Susan Hagen Nipp. "Hickory Dickory Dock" from *Wee Sing*. Price Stern Sloan, 1986.

Glazer, Tom. "Hickory Dickory Dock" from *Tom Glazer Sings Winnie the Pooh and Mother Goose*. Gateway Records/RTV Communications Group, Inc., 1991.

Various Performers. "Hickory Dickory Dock" from *Disney's Children's Favorites, Vol. 4*. Walt Disney Records, 1990.

Various Performers. "Hickory Dickory Dock" from *Kiddin' Around*. Music for Little People, 1991.

TLC10064 Copyright © Teaching & Learning Company, Carthage, IL 62321

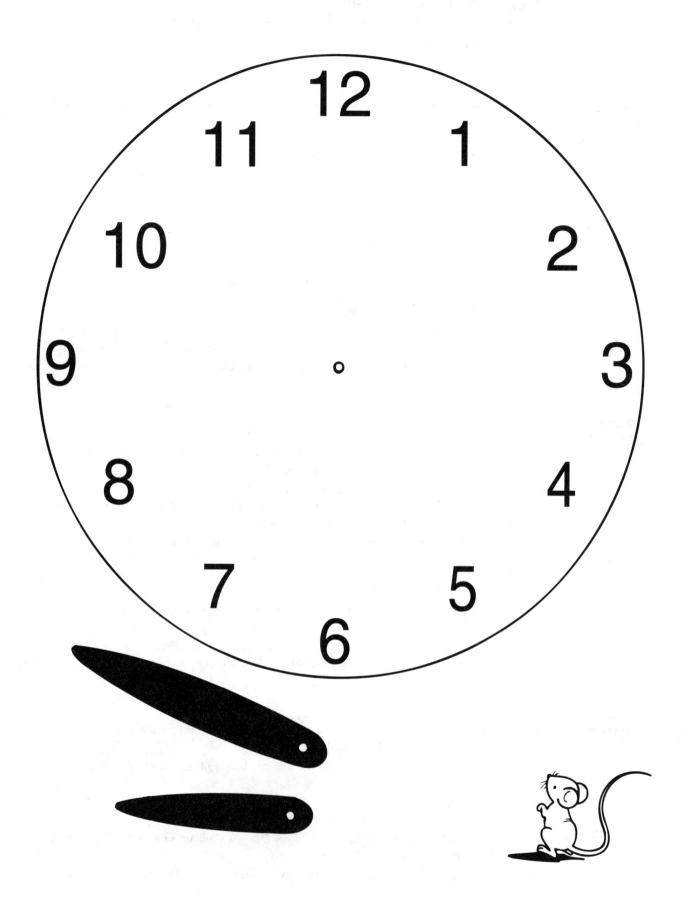

TLC10064 Copyright © Teaching & Learning Company, Carthage, IL 62321

TLC10064 Copyright © Teaching & Learning Company, Carthage, IL 62321

Hot Cross Buns

Hot cross buns!
Hot cross buns!
One a penny, two a penny,
Hot cross buns!
If your daughters do not like them,
Give them to your sons.
One a penny, two a penny,
Hot cross buns!

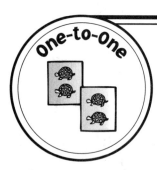

Props/Visual Aids
Cut out and color 10 hot cross buns for each child, using the patterns on page 52. Number each set of buns with the numerals 1 to 10. Provide a bag of 10 pennies for each child.

Talk About
Give each child a set of 10 numbered buns and a bag of pennies. As you sing the song, vary the amount of pennies in the chorus. Ask the children to place pennies on the buns to match the number sung in the song. For "five a penny," the children would count five buns and match them with five pennies.

To Extend This Circle Time
Make hot cross buns using refrigerator rolls in a tube. Follow the package directions for baking. After they have cooled, have the children add hot crosses with decorator frosting in a tube or a simple powdered sugar glaze. Put one cross on each bun. Ask, "How many buns will we need so every child can have one? How many crosses do we need to make?"

Props/Visual Aids
Make a simple salt/flour dough. The children will enjoy helping measure and mix the ingredients. Try this simple recipe.

Simple Dough

3 cups (720 ml) flour
1 cup (240 ml) salt
1 cup (240 ml) water
½ cup (120 ml) vegetable oil
food coloring (optional)

Mix the flour and salt together in a bowl. Slowly add the water, oil and food coloring. Knead the dough well and shape into balls. Store in a tightly closed container or plastic bag and refrigerate. Give each child a small lump of the dough.

TLC10064 Copyright © Teaching & Learning Company, Carthage, IL 62321

Talk About

As you sing the song, invite the children to make small buns from their dough. Ask, "Can you make two buns? Can you make three?"

To Extend This Circle Time

Set up a bakery in your dramatic play area. Provide the children with aprons, chef hats, modeling dough, rolling pins, cookie cutters and pans.

Relationships

Props/Visual Aids

Enlarge the bun patterns on page 52. Make several buns in various colors and cut each into several pieces.

Talk About

Ask, "Which pieces go together?" Have the children put the parts of buns together to make whole buns.

To Extend This Circle Time

Purchase some authentic hot cross buns from a bakery or grocery store. Enjoy the buns at snack time and ask for the children's reactions. "Has anybody eaten hot cross buns before? Do the boys like them more or less than the girls? Which is your favorite part, the cross or the bun?" Graph the class's responses.

Books to Share

Chandra, Deborah. *Miss Mabel's Table*. Harcourt Brace & Company, 1994.
Bright acrylic paintings and a cumulative counting rhyme present the ingredients and techniques that Miss Mabel uses at her restaurant to cook pancakes for 10 people.

Curtis, Neil. *How Bread Is Made*. Lerner Publications Company, 1992.
Simple text and clear photographs describe how bread is made, beginning in a field of wheat and ending at a bakery.

McMillan, Bruce. *Eating Fractions*. Scholastic, Inc., 1991.
Colorful photos illustrate two children's food cut into halves, quarters and thirds and how those parts make a whole.

Morris, Ann. *Bread, Bread, Bread*. Lothrop, Lee & Shepard Books, 1989.
Clear photographs and text celebrate the many different kinds of bread and how they may be enjoyed.

Wolff, Ferida. *Seven Loaves of Bread*. Tambourine Books, 1993.
When Milly, who does the baking on the farm, gets sick, Rose discovers that there are very good reasons for making extra loaves of bread to share with their animals and friends.

Tapes and CDs

Glazer, Tom. "Hot Cross Buns" from *Tom Glazer Sings Winnie the Pooh and Mother Goose*. Gateway Records/RTV Communications Group, Inc., 1991.

TLC10064 Copyright © Teaching & Learning Company, Carthage, IL 62321

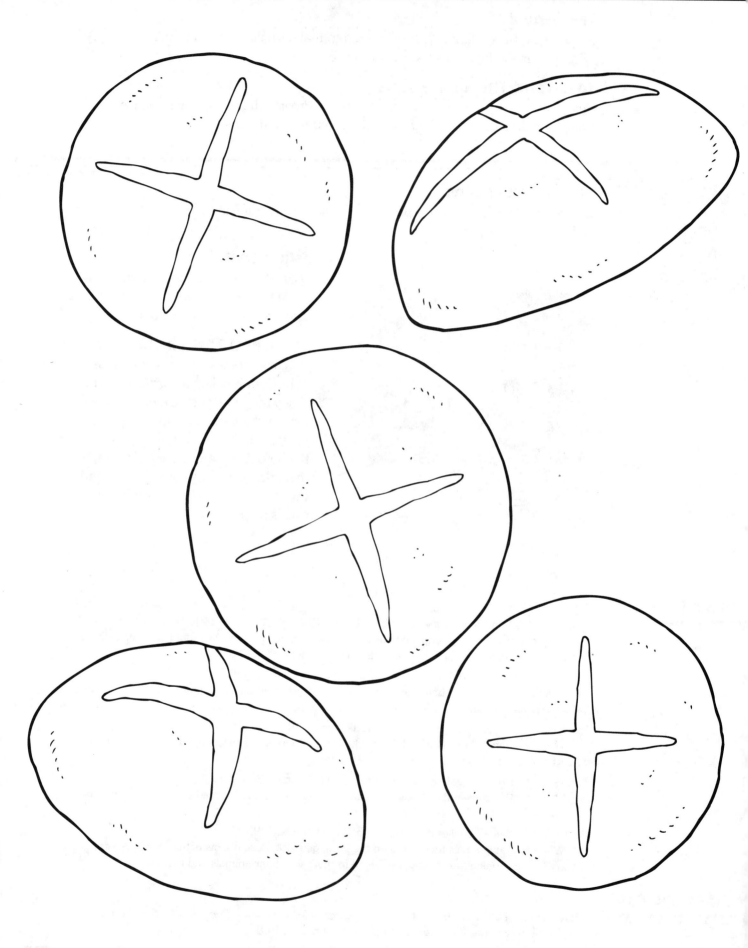

TLC10064 Copyright © Teaching & Learning Company, Carthage, IL 62321

How Much Is That Doggie in the Window?

How much is that doggie in the window?
The one with the waggly tail,
How much is that doggie in the window?
I do hope that doggie's for sale.

Compare/Classify

Props/Visual Aids
Ask each child to bring a stuffed dog or other animal. Find pictures of a variety of types of dogs.

Talk About
Have the children compare the dogs. Ask, "Which are little? Which are big?" Separate the dogs into groups of short-haired and long-haired dogs. Classify the dogs by asking, "Which are spaniels? Which are beagles?"

To Extend This Circle Time
Provide a variety of books with pictures of various dog breeds. (See "Books to Share" on page 56.) Invite your community veterinarian or a local dog breeder to visit your class and talk about the characteristics of different types of dogs.

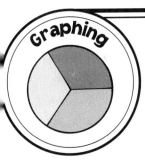
Graphing

Props/Visual Aids
Create a large chart.

Talk About
Ask the children what pets they have at home. If a child does not have a pet, ask what kind he or she would like to have. Give each child a paper cut-out, using the patterns on pages 57 and 58, to represent his or her pet. Make a group chart graphing the number of different types of pets.

TLC10064 Copyright © Teaching & Learning Company, Carthage, IL 62321

Our Pets

🐰	🐰				
🐱	🐱	🐱	🐱		
🐦	🐦				
🐕	🐕	🐕			
🐢					
🐟	🐟				

To Extend This Circle Time

Have the children poll other classrooms or staff in your building to add to the class-room graph. Discuss "What is the most popular pet? What is the least popular pet? What is the most unusual pet?" Set up a pet store in your dramatic play area. Ask parents to bring in items they use for their pets at home. If necessary, use a dish-washer to sanitize them. Invite the children to bring their family pets to the class-room for a short visit. Be sure to check whether any classmates have allergies to specific animals.

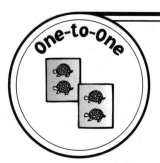

Props/Visual Aids

Supply a box of dog biscuits. Give each child a paper or stuffed dog to hold. You may use the patterns on page 59.

Talk About

Have the children take turns passing out dog biscuits to each dog. Place three dogs in the center of the group. Ask, "How many dog biscuits do we need?" Repeat, varying the number until each child has had a turn counting out biscuits.

TLC10064 Copyright © Teaching & Learning Company, Carthage, IL 62321

To Extend This Circle Time

Make real dog biscuits as a group cooking experience. The children may measure and mix the ingredients. This recipe is from *The Frugal Gourmet Whole Family Cookbook* by Jeff Smith, Avon Books, 1992.

Dog Biscuits

1½ cups (360 ml) barley flour
(found in health food stores)
2 T. (30 ml) bonemeal powder
(also found in health food
stores)
½ tsp. (2.5 ml) salt

2 tsp. (10 ml) baking soda
1½ T. (22 ml) vegetable oil
1 egg yolk
½ cup (120 ml) milk
2 T. (30 ml) honey

Cream the dry ingredients together with the oil. In a separate bowl, beat together the egg yolk, milk and honey. Gradually mix into the dry ingredients. Knead into a dough. Roll the dough out on a lightly floured surface to about ½" (1.25 cm) thick. Cut into any shape you like. (You may also find bone-shaped cutters at a gourmet food shop.) Prick the bones with a fork and place on a greased cookie sheet. Bake in a preheated oven at 375°F (190°C) for about 20 minutes. Turn once to brown evenly.

Patterning

Props/Visual Aids

Cut out pictures of a variety of dogs, either using the patterns on page 59 or creating your own. The dogs should vary by size, shape and color. A small piece of masking tape on the back of the pieces will help them adhere to your flannel board or easel. Make copies of page 60 showing rows of dog outlines. Children can reproduce the pattern shown on the flannel board by coloring the dogs on paper. Encourage the class to create their own patterns.

Talk About

Create a simple pattern such as brown dog, black dog, brown dog, black dog, brown dog. Ask the children to finish the pattern on the flannel board. The patterns may be simple or complex depending on the age of your group. Invite children to create patterns for the rest of the class to complete. Give each child a large plush or paper dog. Have the children hold the dogs in front of them to create a large pattern of dogs.

To Extend This Circle Time
Have the children create stuffed dogs using brown paper bags (either lunch or grocery size), newspapers, construction paper scraps, markers, glue and scissors. Use these dogs for patterning.

Sorting

Props/Visual Aids
Ask each child to bring a stuffed dog or other animal.

Talk About
Sort the animals by color and count the number in each group. Ask, "Which has more? Which has less?"

To Extend This Circle Time
At the math center, provide small plastic animals for the children to sort into plastic bowls or small boxes.

Books to Share

Henry, Marguerite. *Album of Dogs*. Rand McNally, 1970.
    Briefly discusses the history and characteristics of 26 common dog breeds. Illustrated by Wesley Dennis.

Gwynne, Fred. *Easy to See Why*. Simon & Schuster Books for Young Readers, 1993.
    As she walks to the dog show with her beloved mutt, a little girl meets several dogs and their look-alike owners.

Leichman, Seymour. *Shaggy Dogs & Spotty Dogs & Shaggy & Spotty Dogs*. Harcourt Brace Jovanovich, 1973.
    Describes "dogs that sing unlikely notes and dogs who wear plaid overcoats" and many other kinds of dogs.

Tapes and CDs

Jackson, Mike and Michele. "How Much Is That Doggie in the Window?" from *Bunyips, Bunnies and Brumbies*. Elephant Records, 1980.

Sharon, Lois and Bram. "How Much Is That Doggie in the Window?" from *Great Big Hits*. A&M Records, Inc., 1992.

Sharon, Lois and Bram. "How Much Is That Doggie in the Window?" from *Stay Tuned*. Elephant Records, 1987.

TLC10064 Copyright © Teaching & Learning Company, Carthage, IL 62321

TLC10064 Copyright © Teaching & Learning Company, Carthage, IL 62321

58

TLC10064 Copyright © Teaching & Learning Company, Carthage, IL 62321

TLC10064 Copyright © Teaching & Learning Company, Carthage, IL 62321

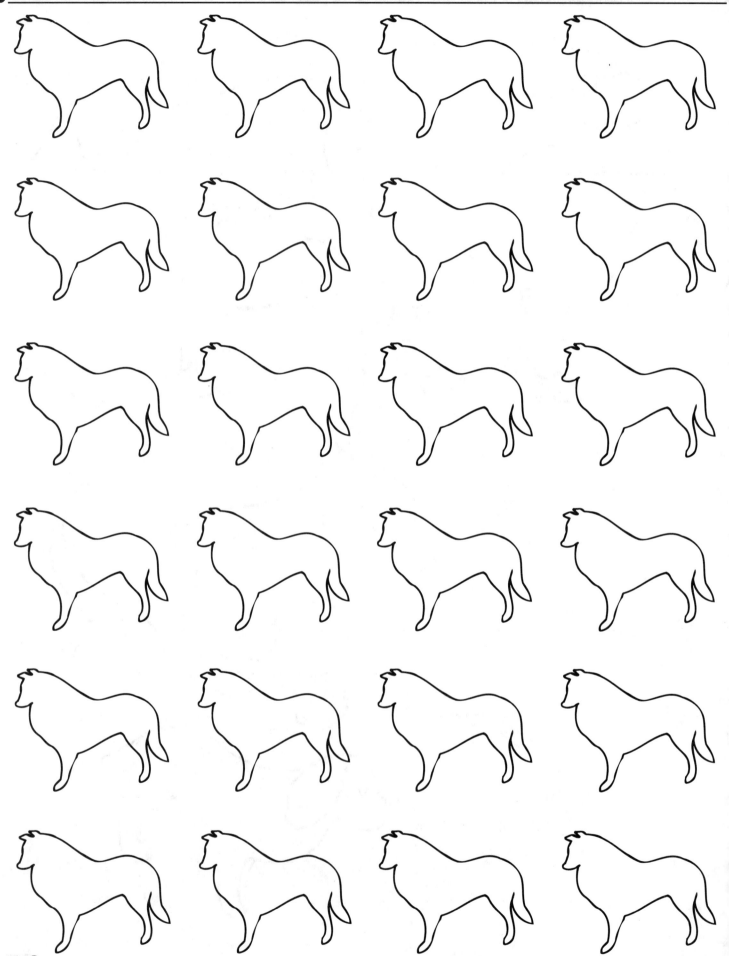

60

TLC10064 Copyright © Teaching & Learning Company, Carthage, IL 62321

One, Two, Buckle My Shoe

One, two, buckle my shoe.
Three, four, shut the door.
Five, six, pick up sticks.
Seven, eight, lay them straight.
Nine, ten, a big fat hen. or (Let's do it again!)

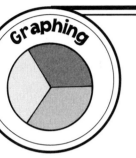

Props/Visual Aids

Ask each child to put one of his or her shoes in the center of the circle.

Talk About

On chart paper, make a bar graph for the shoes. On the bottom of the graph, draw simple representations of the different types of shoes. Invite the children to help you decide the categories: you may have tie shoes, buckle, slip-ons, Velcro™ closures, sandals and boots. Count and record the number of shoes in each category. On another sheet of paper, create a bar graph showing the colors of the shoes.

Our Shoe Colors				
Blue	White	Brown	Black	Other

To Extend This Circle Time

Provide the art center with shoe catalogs or pages from shoe advertisements, safety scissors, glue and paper. Sort the shoes into the different styles and make a collage of each. When the collages are complete, create another bar graph to represent the shoes (style and number of shoes) that the children found in the catalogs.

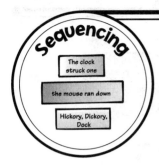

Props/Visual Aids

Write the words to the song on large strips of paper, one phrase per strip.

> **Three, four, shut the door.**

> **Seven, eight, lay them straight.**

> **One, two, buckle my shoe.**

Talk About

Mix up the strips and sing the song with the phrases in a different order. You might sing, "Three, four, shut the door. Seven, eight, lay them straight. One, two, buckle my shoe." Display the strips (taped to flannel or chalkboard) as you sing them out of order; then ask the children to help you find the correct sequence.

To Extend This Circle Time

Encourage the children to help you write new words to the song, following the same number sequences. Focus on a unit theme you are studying, an approaching holiday or everyday classroom events. You might sing:

> "One, two, a valentine for you.
> Three, four, let's make some more.
> Five, six, here's paint we can mix.
> Seven, eight, that color looks great.
> Nine, ten, give it to a friend."

Try the sequencing activity with the children's new words.

Props/Visual Aids

Enlarge the number patterns for numerals 1 to 10 (pages 64 and 65). Reproduce on colored paper, cut out and laminate for durability.

Talk About

Give the numbers to different children and ask them to hold their numbers high when the numbers are sung. Be sure to sing the song several times so that every child has a chance to hold a number. Try this activity first with the numerals and children in order around the circle. Then mix them up for a more challenging activity!

To Extend This Circle Time

Share several of the terrific counting books available from your library. Provide each child with a large numeral from the patterns on pages 64 and 65, washable markers and stickers to create your own class counting book.

TLC10064 Copyright © Teaching & Learning Company, Carthage, IL 62321

Sorting

Props/Visual Aids
Purchase multicolored straws and cut into several lengths or use strips of colored paper cut into several lengths. Cover several shoe boxes with the same color paper as the straws or strips.

Talk About
Give each child five strips of the colored paper. Place the colored boxes in the center of the circle and ask the children to sort their strips by color into the matching boxes. To sort by length, use a large box and a small box. Give the children two different lengths of the same color strips to sort. For a more advanced activity, use strips in different colors to sort by length.

To Extend This Circle Time
Supply a variety of pasta shapes. You might have bows, wheels, elbow macaroni and tubes. Have the children sort the pasta by shape. Place spaghetti noodles in a paper bag with a small amount of powdered tempera paint. Shake the bag to color the noodles. Break the spaghetti into different lengths and sort by color or length.

Books to Share

Burton, Marilee Robin. *My Best Shoes*. Tambourine Books, 1994.
Vibrant paintings and playful rhyme celebrate the variety of shoes worn by a multicultural cast of children throughout a busy week.

Katz, Michael Jay. *Ten Potatoes in a Pot and Other Counting Rhymes*. Harper & Row, 1990.
Classic illustrations combine with 24 traditional counting rhymes, including both popular and little-known verses.

Miller, Margaret. *Whose Shoe?* Greenwillow Books, 1991.
Colorful photographs and very simple text illustrate a variety of footwear and matches each wearer with the appropriate shoe.

Morris, Ann. *Shoes, Shoes, Shoes*. Lothrop, Lee & Shepard Books, 1995.
Bright, interesting photographs and simple rhyming text describe all kinds of shoes: some for dancing, walking, playing; some for snow or ice; some made of wood or cloth.

Williams, Jenny. *One, Two, Buckle My Shoe*. Dial Books for Young Readers, 1987.
A collection of 12 counting rhymes for young children including "Ten in the Bed" and "Five Little Ducks."

Winthrop, Elizabeth. *Shoes*. Harper & Row, 1986. Bright, humorous illustrations and rhyming verse describe many kinds of shoes but conclude the best are your own bare feet.

Tapes and CDs

Jenkins, Ella. "One, Two, Buckle My Shoe" from *Counting Games & Rhymes for Little Ones*. Folkways Records, 1965.

Various Performers. "One, Two, Buckle My Shoe" from *Disney's Children's Favorites, Vol. 3*. Walt Disney Records, 1986.

64

TLC10064 Copyright © Teaching & Learning Company, Carthage, IL 62321

TLC10064 Copyright © Teaching & Learning Company, Carthage, IL 62321

Peter Hammers

Peter hammers with one hammer,
One hammer, one hammer.
Peter hammers with one hammer,
all day long.
(additional verses)
Two hammers
Three hammers
Four hammers
Five hammers
Very tired now
Wide awake now

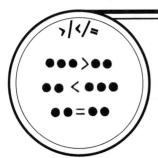

Props/Visual Aids
Use the card patterns on page 69. Color in dots on the cards to show the numbers 1 to 5 or 1 to 10, depending on the skill level of your group.

Talk About
Show the class a card. Count the dots together and sing the song's verse using that number. Then show the class another card and count the dots. Ask, "Are there more, less or the same number of dots on this card?" Sing that verse of the song and repeat with a new card.

To Extend This Circle Time
Invite a local builder or carpenter to visit your class. Before the visit, talk about what things the carpenter might build and what tools he or she uses. Toolboxes, usually off-limits for safety reasons, are fascinating to children. Ask the carpenter to demonstrate as many tools and their uses as possible.

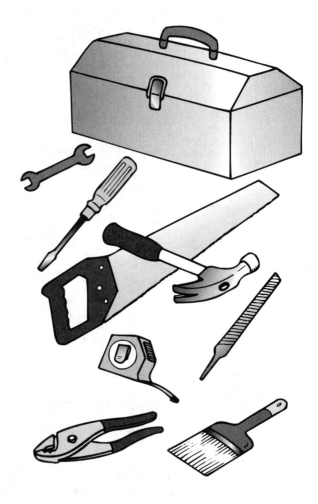

TLC10064 Copyright © Teaching & Learning Company, Carthage, IL 62321

Patterning

Props/Visual Aids
Reproduce the hammer pattern on page 69. Make 25 hammers, each set of five a different color. Laminate for durability.

Talk About
As you sing the song, change the verses to indicate a color. You might sing, "Peter hammers with blue hammers, blue hammers, blue hammers . . . " Place the blue hammer on the flannel board. Ask a child to add another colored hammer to the board as everyone sings the new verse. As a pattern is created on the flannel board, continue to sing the song, matching the colors.

To Extend This Circle Time
Place Styrofoam™ blocks, colored golf tees and small hammers in your building block area. Ask the children to create patterns by hammering the colored golf tees into the Styrofoam™. You may want to use the card patterns on page 69. Color the dots to make patterns for the children to duplicate, or ask them to color the cards to show you patterns they have created.

Prenumber

Props/Visual Aids
Bring to class 15 hammers, real and/or toy, or make copies of the hammer pattern on page 69.

Talk About
As you sing the song, ask a child to count out the hammers needed for that verse. Place the hammers for each verse together in a group. Sing the song several times if needed, so every child has a chance to count out the specified number of hammers for a verse.

To Extend This Circle Time

Sing the song, changing the name *Peter* to the name of a child in your group. As each child's name is sung, that child can demonstrate an action for that verse. You might have:

>one hammer–child pounds with one fist
>two hammers–child pounds with both fists
>three hammers–child pounds with both fists and one foot
>four hammers–child pounds with both fists and both feet
>five hammers–child pounds with both fists and feet and nods head
>very tired now–child pretends to sleep
>wide awake now–child leaps up and dances

Encourage the children to think of new ways to show each number in the song. They might use knees, elbows, fingers or noses to be their "hammers"!

Props/Visual Aids

Reproduce the tool patterns on page 70. Make five of each type of tool and color in various colors. Cut out and laminate for durability.

Talk About

Vary the words of the song to include the names of other tools. You might sing, "Peter saws with one hand . . . " or "Peter turns his screwdriver . . ." Give each child several different tool cards and invite them to place the cards in piles as you sing about each tool.

To Extend This Circle Time

Set up a woodworking center in your classroom. You may be able to locate simple child-size tools at a local hardware store. Many school suppliers sell children's tool sets. Safety glasses must also be purchased and used at all times. Invite a parent with an interest in woodworking to help you get started.

Books to Share

Florian, Douglas. *A Carpenter.* Greenwillow Books, 1991.
>Simple text and watercolor illustrations describe a carpenter's work and the tools he uses.

Kelley, True. *Hammers and Mops, Pencils and Pots.* Crown Publishers, 1994.
>Detailed and labeled illustrations describe various kinds of tools and implements used in the kitchen, garden, workshop, office and other settings.

Morris, Ann. *Tools.* Lothrop, Lee & Shepard Books, 1992.
>Colorful photographs and simple text introduce tools from all over the world and the people who use them.

Rockwell, Anne, and Harlow Rockwell. *The Toolbox.* Macmillan, 1971.
>A child describes the tools in his father's toolbox and how they are used.

Tapes and CDs

Monet, Lisa. "Peter Hammers" from *Jump Down.* Circle Sound Productions, 1987.

TLC10064 Copyright © Teaching & Learning Company, Carthage, IL 62321

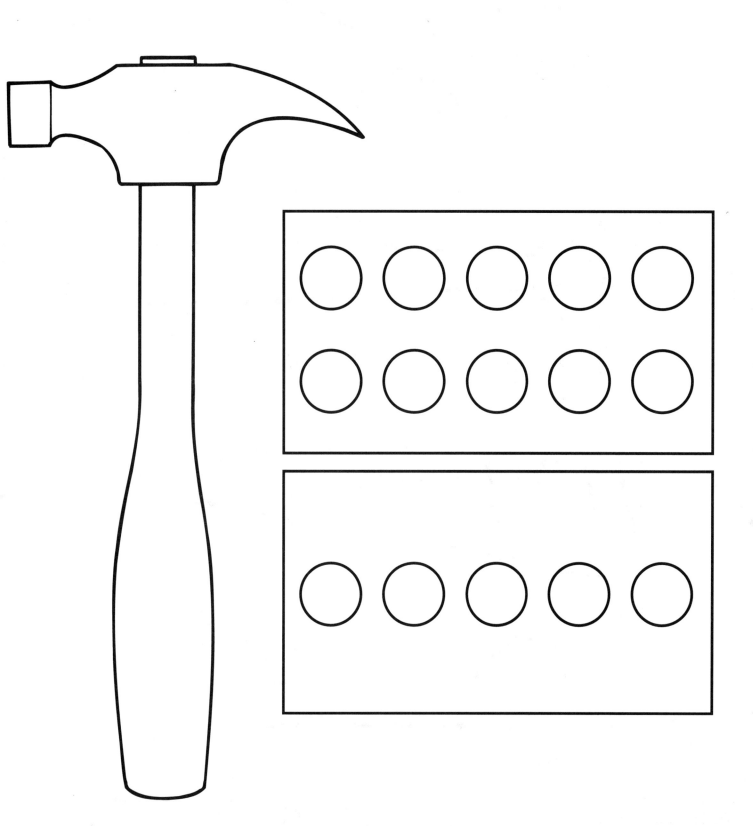

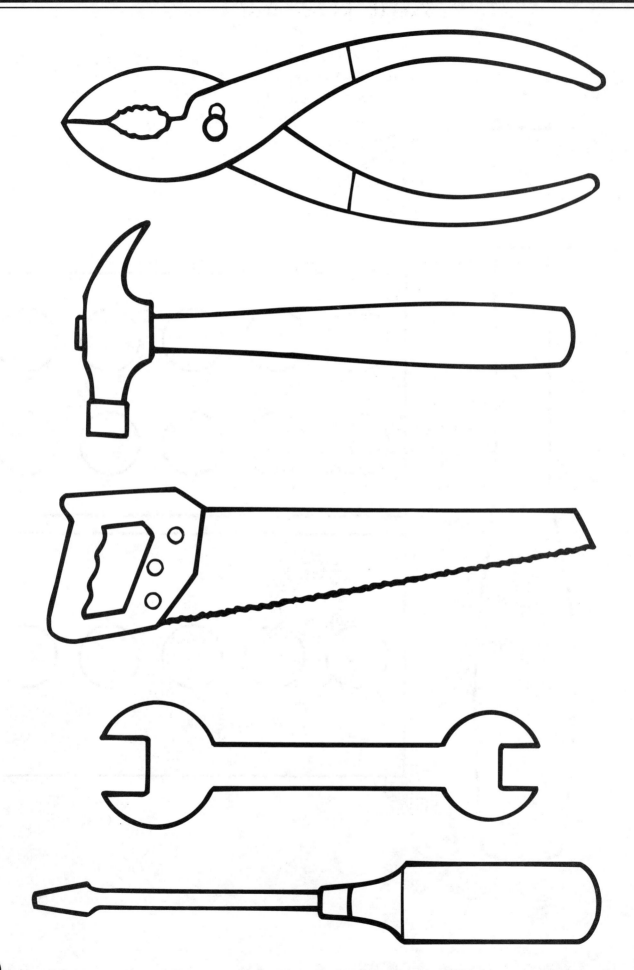

70

TLC10064 Copyright © Teaching & Learning Company, Carthage, IL 62321

Roll the Ball

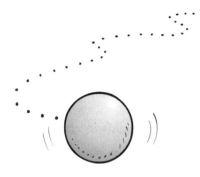

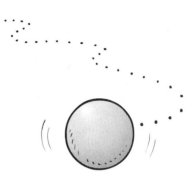

I roll the ball to Daddy,
He rolls it back to me.
I roll the ball to Mommy,
She rolls it back to me.
Roll the ball, roll the ball,
Roll the ball, roll the ball,
I roll the ball to Daddy,
He rolls it back to me.

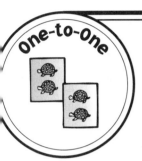

One-to-One

Props/Visual Aids
You will need five playground or soft, foam balls.

Talk About
Have the children sit in a circle, cross-legged. As you sing the song, roll a ball to one child, who will then roll it to another child. As the children understand the game, add a second, third, fourth and fifth ball, continuing to roll one at a time.

To Extend This Circle Time
Gather the children around a parachute or large bedsheet. Place the balls one at a time in the center of the parachute. Have the children gently shake the parachute as you sing the song. Continue adding balls.

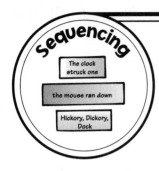

Sequencing

The clock struck one

the mouse ran down

Hickory, Dickory, Dock

Props/Visual Aids

You will need a large playgound ball. Write the names of the children on slips of paper and place them in a basket.

Talk About

Have the children sit in a circle. One at a time, draw three names from the basket. Read the names aloud emphasizing the order in which you drew them. Have those children roll the ball to each other in the correct sequence. Repeat this activity with other sets of names. As the children's skill increases, add more names to the sequence.

To Extend This Circle Time

Take this game outside to your playground area. Stand in a circle and take turns throwing and then kicking the ball in sequence.

Seriation

3 2 1

Props/Visual Aids

You will need a variety of sizes of balls or use a copy machine to enlarge and reduce one of the ball patterns on page 74.

Talk About

If using the ball patterns, give each child three balls of varying size. Ask, "Can you find which of your balls is the smallest? Which is next smallest?" Have the children place their balls in order smallest to largest. Try the activity as a group with real balls. "Which kind of ball is the smallest? Who has the golf balls?" Make a line of balls, smallest to largest, in the center of your circle.

To Extend This Circle Time

Give each child a lump of modeling dough. Invite the children to roll the dough into differently sized balls and place the balls in order from smallest to largest. You might try this activity with prepared cookie dough. Have the children form balls with the chilled dough. Place the balls of dough on the cookie sheets according to size. Ask, "Do you think the cookies will be different sizes after they are baked? Which will be the biggest cookie? Smallest?"

TLC10064 Copyright © Teaching & Learning Company, Carthage, IL 62321

Sorting

Props/Visual Aids
Bring in many different types of balls, or if necessary, use the patterns on page 74 for sorting.

Talk About
As you sing the song, roll out different types of balls. Ask, "What kind of ball is this? What would you use it for?" Have the children sort the balls several times by shape, size and color.

To Extend This Circle Time
Use the different types of balls in your gymnasium or playground. Add a ball pit to your classroom, available commercially or use a plastic swimming pool to hold the balls. Ask the children to sort the balls in the pit by color. Take a field trip to an indoor playground with a large ball pit.

Books to Share

Bang, Molly. *Yellow Ball.* Morrow Junior Books, 1991.
A yellow ball, forgotten after a game at the beach, drifts out to sea and after some adventures, finds a safe, new home.

Gemme, Leila Boyle. *Soccer Is Our Game.* Children's Press, 1979.
Bright photographs and simple text introduce the game of soccer.

Lillegard, Dee. *My Yellow Ball.* Dutton Children's Books, 1993.
Five times, when a girl throws her yellow ball, her imagination takes it far away to jungles, deserts and outer space, but it always returns.

Saltzberg, Barney. *Mrs. Morgan's Lawn.* Hyperion Books for Children, 1993.
Mrs. Morgan is very protective of her immaculate front yard and confiscates all the soccer balls, baseballs and other kinds of balls that land there while the neighborhood children are playing.

Yardley, Joanna. *The Red Ball.* Harcourt Brace Jovanovich, 1991.
When Joanie searches for her red ball, she finds it in an old photograph and follows it from photo to photo, until the past unites with the present.

Tapes and CDs

Rhino. *Red Rubber Ball* by The Cyrcle. Kid Rock.

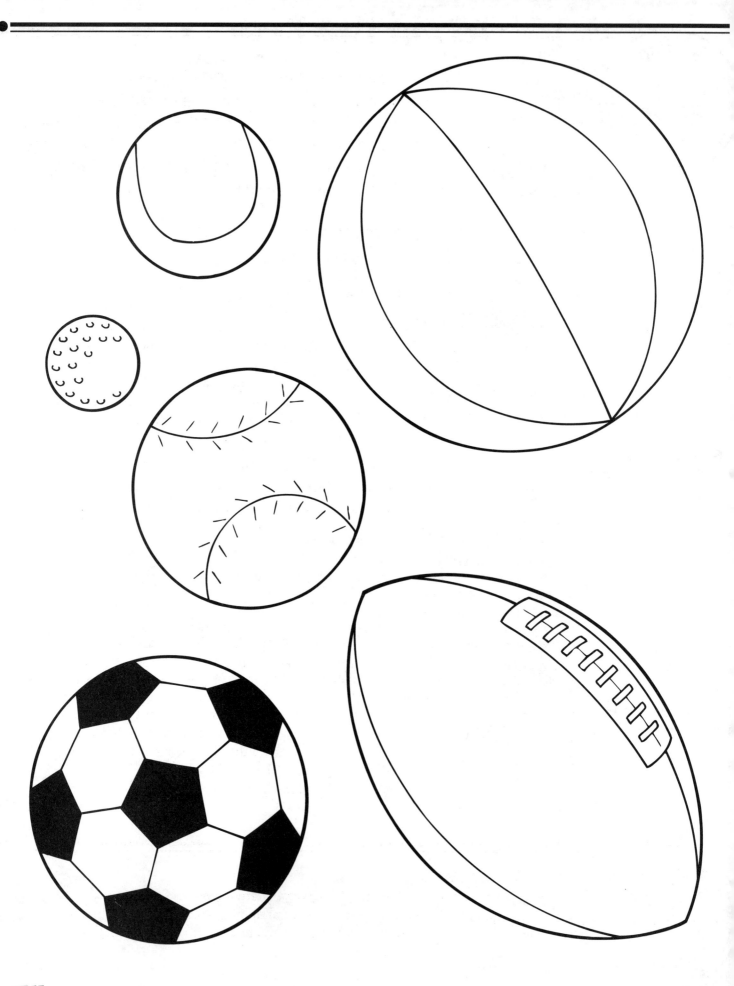

TLC10064 Copyright © Teaching & Learning Company, Carthage, IL 62321

Ten in the Bed

There were ten in the bed
And the little one said
"Roll over, roll over!"
So they all rolled over
And one fell out.

(Verses continue with nine in the bed, eight in the bed . . . and so on)

Compare/Classify

Props/Visual Aids
Collect a variety of fabric scraps, especially the types used in pajamas. You might find cotton, knit, flannel, nylon and velour.

Talk About
Give each child a small piece of fabric. Pass the pieces around the group so everyone has a chance to touch them. Ask, "Does anyone have pajamas that feel like this fabric? Would you like to have pajamas made from this fabric?" Have the children group the fabric that is soft, fuzzy or shiny.

To Extend This Circle Time
In the art center, provide washable markers or crayons, glue, safety scissors and paper. Use the patterns on page 79 for simple paper dolls; you might first cut out the dolls for younger children. Using small scraps of the pajama fabric and glue, have the children dress their dolls for bed. Some types of fabric may be difficult to cut with safety scissors, so you may want to provide some precut pajama shapes. Ask everyone to wear their pajamas to school for the whole day. (You might ask parents to send some regular clothes in case their child wants to change later in the day.) Ask questions to compare the children's pajamas. "Who has blue pajamas? Whose pajamas have feet? Does anyone have superhero pajamas?"

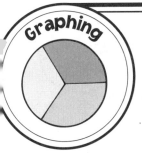

Graphing

Props/Visual Aids
On chart paper, make a picture graph showing different types of beds. You might have a daybed, futon, trundle, twin, double, water and bunk bed. Give each child a card with his or her name on it, or ask the children to write their names on the cards.

TLC10064 Copyright © Teaching & Learning Company, Carthage, IL 62321

Talk About

Sing the song. Ask, "Do you think they had a large bed, to fit 10 in, or a small bed?" Ask the children what kind of bed they sleep in. Show them pictures of different types of beds from catalogs (visit a furniture or bedding store and ask for catalogs showing a variety of beds) or books to help them decide. Ask the children to place their cards on the graph in the section showing their type of bed. Count how many cards are in each section.

Our Beds			
Single	Jon	Kim	Luisa
Double	Pete		
Bunk	Juan	Tony	

To Extend This Circle Time

Ask parents to bring a photograph showing their child's bed. Display them on a bulletin board or poster. Set up your dramatic play area as a bedroom. Bring in a cot or borrow a trundle bed. Add a reading lamp, posters, books, plants, stuffed animals and anything else you can think of to make the area seem "homey."

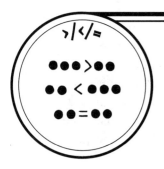

Props/Visual Aids

Use the patterns on page 80 to make 10 bunnies. Color and laminate for durability. Attach a piece of tape, sandpaper or flannel to the back so it will adhere to the flannel board. Make a large bed frame from construction paper or felt to use on the flannel board.

TLC10064 Copyright © Teaching & Learning Company, Carthage, IL 62321

Talk About

Place most of the bunnies on the bed and the rest beside the bed. Have the children count the number of bunnies in the bed and the number out of the bed. Ask, "Where are most of the bunnies?" As you sing the song, move the figures, stopping to count each time. "When are there as many in the bed as out of the bed? When will there be more out of the bed?"

To Extend This Circle Time

Bring in mats, cots or bath towels for each student to lie on. As you sing the song, invite the students to "roll over." Then count the number of children still on their mats and the number on the floor. Ask, "Are there more children on mats or more on the floor?" Be prepared to repeat this activity many times!

Props/Visual Aids

Use the patterns on pages 80 and 81 to make 10 bunnies and 10 bears. Color and laminate for durability. Attach a piece of tape, sandpaper or flannel to the back so it will adhere to the flannel board. Make a large bed frame from construction paper or felt to use on the flannel board.

Talk About

Sing the song with 10 of the bunnies and bears in the bed arranged in a simple pattern. You might have bunny, bear, bear, bunny, bear, bear and so on. Keep the extra figures close by to allow for a variety of patterns. Start another simple pattern and ask the children to complete it.

To Extend This Circle Time

Make a class quilt. Quilting is a wonderful activity that involves patterning. Give each child a square of white paper. Supply the art center with small circles, squares and triangles of brightly colored construction paper. Invite the children to glue a design on their white paper. When the squares are dry, lay out the pattern for the quilt on the floor. Use squares of solid-color construction paper interspersed with the children's designs to create patterns of design and solid squares. Tape the quilt squares together with masking tape on the back. You can also make a quilt using fabric squares. Have the children, or each child's family, make a design using fabric crayons, embroidery floss, fabric paint, appliqué or whatever they choose. Sew the squares together and display your quilt as a colorful wall hanging.

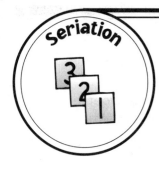

Seriation

Props/Visual Aids

Bring a variety of sizes of dolls and stuffed animals and a wooden doll bed. Use the patterns on pages 82 to 86. Color and laminate for durablility.

Talk About

Have the children help you place the dolls and animals on the doll bed in order from smallest to largest. Sing the song and invite the children to help the tallest animal or doll fall out of the bed first and the smallest last. Place the 10 bears in various sizes on the floor or flannel board, and ask the children to arrange them in order by size. For younger children, begin with fewer bears and with more obvious differences in size.

To Extend This Circle Time

Have the class act out the song. Line the children up to determine the order of tallest to smallest. Or you might ask them to sit on the floor with their backs against the wall to measure whose legs are the longest. Use your circle time rug or other carpeted area as the bed. As the children "fall out," they may join the circle around the bed to continue singing until the smallest child has "fallen" and the song is finished.

Books to Share

Cleary, Beverly. *Janet's Thingamajigs.* William Morrow & Company, Inc., 1987.
Four-year-old Janet creates envy in her twin brother Jimmy by hoarding special treasures in her crib, until the arrival of real beds reminds them that they are both growing up.

Freedman, Sally. *Devin's New Bed.* Albert Whitman & Company, 1986.
Devin is reluctant to give up his crib and accept his new grown-up bed, until he discovers how much fun the new bed can be.

Hennessey, B.G. *Sleep Tight.* Viking, 1992.
Luminous illustrations and simple rhyming text describe two sleepy children and how everything around them is ready for the quiet nighttime.

Jonas, Ann. *The Quilt.* Greenwillow Books, 1984.
A child's beautiful new patchwork quilt recalls old memories and provides new adventures at bedtime.

Rees, Mary. *Ten in a Bed.* Little, Brown and Company, 1988.
Humorous and detailed drawings follow the antics of nine friends and the little girl who pushed them all out of bed in this familiar counting rhyme.

Roth, Susan L. *Patchwork Tales.* Atheneum, 1984.
Illustrated with wood block prints of quilt patches, a grandmother tells her granddaughter the family stories behind the various blocks in a patchwork quilt.

Wood, Audrey. *The Napping House.* Harcourt Brace Jovanovich, 1984.
Colorful paintings illustrate this cumulative tale about a wakeful flea atop a number of sleeping creatures and the commotion it caused with just one bite.

Ziefert, Harriet. *I Want to Sleep in Your Bed!* Harper & Row, 1990.
When Susan wants to sleep in her parents' bed, she and her mom take a nighttime walk to see everyone sleeping in their own beds.

Tapes and CDs

Beall, Pamela Conn, and Susan Hagen Nipp. "Ten in a Bed" from *Wee Sing Silly Songs.* Price Stern Sloan, 1986.

Monet, Lisa. "Roll Over" from *Jump Down.* Music for Little People, 1987.

Penner, Fred. "10 in the Bed" from *Fred Penner's Place.* Oak Street Music, 1988.

Scruggs, Joe. "Whole Bed" from *Bahamas Pajamas.* Educational Graphics Press, 1990.

Sharon, Lois and Bram. "Ten in the Bed" from *Sharon, Lois & Bram's Elephant Show Record.* Elephant Records/A&M Records, 1986.

TLC10064 Copyright © Teaching & Learning Company, Carthage, IL 62321

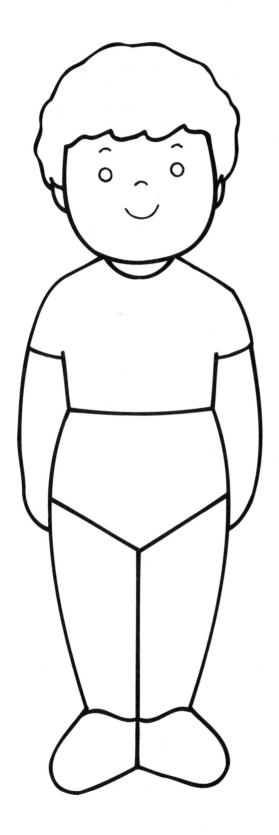
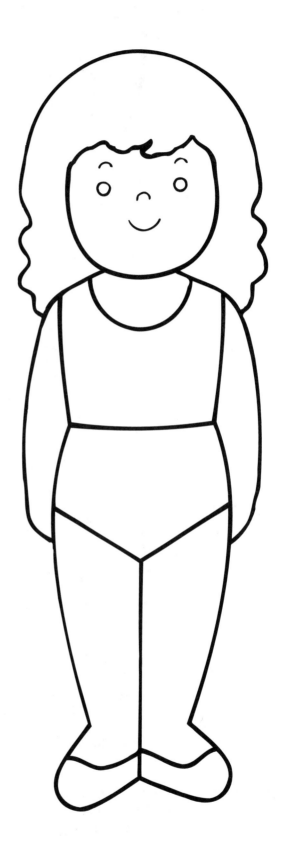

TLC10064 Copyright © Teaching & Learning Company, Carthage, IL 62321

80

TLC10064 Copyright © Teaching & Learning Company, Carthage, IL 62321

TLC10064 Copyright © Teaching & Learning Company, Carthage, IL 62321

TLC10064 Copyright © Teaching & Learning Company, Carthage, IL 62321

TLC10064 Copyright © Teaching & Learning Company, Carthage, IL 62321

84

TLC10064 Copyright © Teaching & Learning Company, Carthage, IL 62321

TLC10064 Copyright © Teaching & Learning Company, Carthage, IL 62321

TLC10064 Copyright © Teaching & Learning Company, Carthage, IL 62321

This Old Man

This old man, he played one,
He played knick-knack on my thumb,
(chorus)
With a knick-knack, paddy wack,
Give the dog a bone,
This old man came rolling home.
(verses)
This old man, he played two,
He played knick-knack on my shoe . . .
Three: on my knee
Four: on my door
Five: on my hive
Six: on my sticks
Seven: up in heaven
Eight: on my gate
Nine: on my vine
Ten: all over again

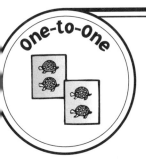

One-to-One

Props/Visual Aids

Dress a puppet or doll to be the old man in the song. Make copies of the patterns on pages 90 and 91 or, if possible, use real items, enough for the corresponding number in the verse. On 10 large sheets of paper draw dots, one on the first page, two on the second and so on with 10 dots spaced on the last sheet. You may choose instead to place round counters on the floor, adding one counter for each verse.

Talk About

Pass out the pattern pieces or real items to the children. Have them count out the pieces and lay them on the counters or dots as you sing the song. Say, "Let's give the old man six sticks. One, two, three, four, five, six. Are there any dots left over? Are there any extra sticks?"

To Extend This Circle Time

Provide a brown, grocery size paper bag for each child. Cut a hole in the top for the child's head and an armhole on each side. Supply the

TLC10064 Copyright © Teaching & Learning Company, Carthage, IL 62321

art center with construction paper scraps, tempera paint and brushes, yarn, washable markers, scissors and glue. Invite the children to create costumes for the items in the song, the old man and the numerals 1 to 10. Wear the costumes as the class sings the song, each character stepping into the circle as his or her part is sung. For each chorus, have the characters in the middle join hands for a circle dance. Invite another class or the children's parents to watch the performance.

Patterning

Props/Visual Aids

Write the words to the song on a large piece of chart paper. You can use the patterns on pages 90 and 91 to add visual cues to the words as the children are learning the song.

Talk About

The words and rhythms in this song make a wonderful pattern. (An important part of learning about patterns is finding them in unexpected places.) Have the children clap hands, snap fingers and stomp feet to the word patterns in the song.

To Extend This Circle Time

Ask the class to help you create actions for the repeating part of the pattern. You might have "This old man" (hands on head); "Knick-knack paddy wack" (fists alternate "pounding" each other or the floor); "Give the dog a bone" (bend down, hand out) and "Came rolling home" (roll arms in a circle in front of you).

TLC10064 Copyright © Teaching & Learning Company, Carthage, IL 62321

Props/Visual Aids

Reproduce the patterns on pages 90 and 91. You will also need a large piece of chart paper and markers.

Talk About

In this song there is a rhyming relationship between the numeral in the verse and the item on which the old man plays knick-knack. Ask the children to find examples in the song and write them on the chart paper. Then ask what other words rhyme with the numerals and record them. Use the new words to create new verses for the song. Remember, silly words are best!

To Extend This Circle Time

Ask the children to search in the classroom for other items that rhyme with the numerals and things in the song. When a rhyming item is found, ask the child to place the related picture from the provided patterns on the classroom item.

Books to Share

Jones, Carol. *This Old Man*. Houghton Mifflin, 1990.
   This familiar song has detailed illustrations and a cut-out circle on each page to focus on the next place this old man will play knick-knack.

Marks, Alan. *Over the Hills and Far Away: A Book of Nursery Rhymes*. North-South Books, 1994.
   Bright paintings illustrate a collection of 60 classic nursery rhymes.

Tapes and CDs

Greg and Steve. "This Old Man" from *Oscar, Bingo, and Buddies*. CMS Records, Inc., 1986.

Monet, Lisa. "This Old Man" from *Circle Time: Songs and Rhymes for the Very Young*. Monet Productions, 1986.

Raffi. "This Old Man" from *Baby Beluga*. Troubadour Records, 1977.

Various Performers. "This Old Man" from *For Our Children*. Walt Disney Records, 1991.

Various Performers. "This Old Man (Knick Knack Paddy Whack)" from *Disney's Children's Favorites, Vol. 1*. Walt Disney Productions, 1979.

TLC10064 Copyright © Teaching & Learning Company, Carthage, IL 62321

Three Little Kittens

Three little kittens,
They lost their mittens,
And they began to cry,
"Oh, Mother dear, we sadly fear,
That we have lost our mittens."
"What, lost your mittens? You naughty kittens!
Then you shall have no pie.
Mee-ow, mee-ow.
Then you shall have no pie."

Three little kittens,
They found their mittens,
And they began to cry,
"Oh, Mother dear, see here, see here,
For we have found our mittens."
"Put on your mittens you silly kittens,
And you shall have some pie."
"Purr-rr, purr-rr,
Oh, let us have some pie."

Three little kittens,
They put on their mittens,
And soon ate up the pie.
"Oh, Mother dear, we greatly fear,
That we have soiled our mittens."
"What, soiled your mittens? You naughty kittens!"
Then they began to sigh,
"Mee-ow, mee-ow."
Then they began to sigh.

Three little kittens,
They washed their mittens,
And hung them out to dry.
"Oh, Mother dear, do you not hear,
That we have washed our mittens?"
"What, washed your mittens?
Then you are good kittens,
But I smell a rat close by."
"Mee-ow, mee-ow,
We smell a rat close by."

TLC10064 Copyright © Teaching & Learning Company, Carthage, IL 62321

Compare/Classify

Props/Visual Aids

Have each child bring in a pair of socks from home. Be sure to inform parents that the socks will get dirty and to label each sock with the child's name. You will need two plastic wash-tubs, one partially filled with damp sand and the other with warm soapy water. Be sure to have towels handy to catch any drips!

Talk About

The mittens in the song are lost, found, soiled, clean, wet and dry. Help the children pull the socks over their hands and arms like mittens. As you sing the song, have the children pretend to be kittens and play in the damp sand to soil their mittens. Ask, "How do the mittens look? How do they feel?" Invite the children to wash the mittens in the warm soapy water. "How do they look now?"

To Extend This Circle Time

Set up a laundry in your dramatic play area. Provide warm, soapy water in a sensory table or plastic tub. Wash doll clothes, dolls, doll dishes and other classroom toys. Hang a clothesline in a safe, nontraffic area and provide nonpinching wooden clothespins.

Patterning

Props/Visual Aids

If you live in a cold climate, have the children bring their mittens into the classroom. You may also use the pattern on page 96. Make at least five pairs of mittens, using different colors or patterned paper for several pairs.

Talk About

Use right-hand mittens to create a simple pattern. Your pattern might be solid red, solid blue, purple stripe. Ask the children to copy the pattern using the left-hand mittens.

To Extend This Circle Time

Supply the art center with a variety of yarn remnants, plastic yarn needles and squares of burlap. You may draw a pattern on the burlap with a marker, or let the children create their own. Help the children thread the needles with yarn. Plastic yarn needles have large holes, making them very easy to thread. The children will love to sew!

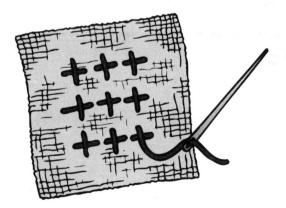

Props/Visual Aids
Use the mitten pattern on page 96 to make pairs of mittens. Color or create different designs, such as stripes or dots, on each pair, and laminate for durability.

Talk About
Give each child one mitten and have the group work together to find each mitten's mate. Ask, "Why do these mittens belong together?"

To Extend This Circle Time
Make pie with your class. You can purchase frozen pie crusts already formed in 8" (20 cm) or individual size pie tins. Graham cracker crusts are also readily available in the 8" (20 cm) or individual sizes. Pour in prepared canned fruit fillings or fill pre-baked crusts with instant pudding. The children will love to take turns making pudding by shaking the milk and powder in a large (over two cups [480 ml]) plastic cup with a tight-fitting lid. Cut strips of the prepared pie dough and have the children crisscross the strips on the fruit pies for a lattice-look top crust. Follow the package directions for baking the pastry crust pies. Enjoy the pie with your class!

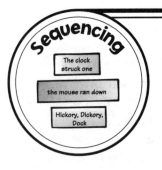

Props/Visual Aids
You will need large chart paper and markers.

TLC10064 Copyright © Teaching & Learning Company, Carthage, IL 62321

Talk About

This is a song that tells a story. It has a definite beginning, middle and end. Sing the song and share one of the children's books that tells the story. (See "Books to Share.") Help the children break the story into different parts. Ask, "What is the first thing that happened? What happened next? What happened at the end of the story?" Draw simple illustrations on the chart paper to provide a visual cue for the song's sequence.

To Extend This Circle Time

Write another ending to the story with your children. "Did they catch the rat? Did the kittens keep their mittens clean?" Invite the children to draw pictures to illustrate the different parts of the story. Arrange the pictures in sequence.

Books to Share

Brett, Jan. *The Mitten*. Putnam, 1989.
Several animals sleep snugly in Nicki's lost mitten until the bear sneezes.

Cauley, Lorinda Bryan. *The Three Little Kittens*. G.P. Putnam's Sons, 1982.
Expressive and delicately colored drawings illustrate this familiar nursery tale.

Galdone, Paul. *Three Little Kittens*. Clarion Books, 1986.
Colorful illustrations help tell the familiar story of the three careless kittens, their mittens and pie.

Polushkin, Maria. *Kitten in Trouble*. Bradbury Press, 1988.
Kitten's day is full of misadventures, described with simple text and refrain and playful illustrations.

Rogers, Jean. *Runaway Mittens*. Greenwillow Books, 1988.
Pica's mittens are always turning up in strange places, but when he finds them keeping the newborn puppies warm in their box, he decides they are in exactly the right place.

Schlein, Miriam. *The Way Mothers Are*. Albert Whitman & Company, 1993.
A little cat tries to figure out why his mother loves him even when he is naughty, and if she loves him at other times because he is good.

Spohn, Kate. *Clementine's Winter Wardrobe*. Orchard Books, 1989.
Clementine the cat chooses the clothes she will need next winter.

Tapes and CDs

Sharon, Lois and Bram. "Three Little Kittens" from *Mainly Mother Goose: Songs and Rhymes for Merry Young Souls*. Elephant Records, 1984.

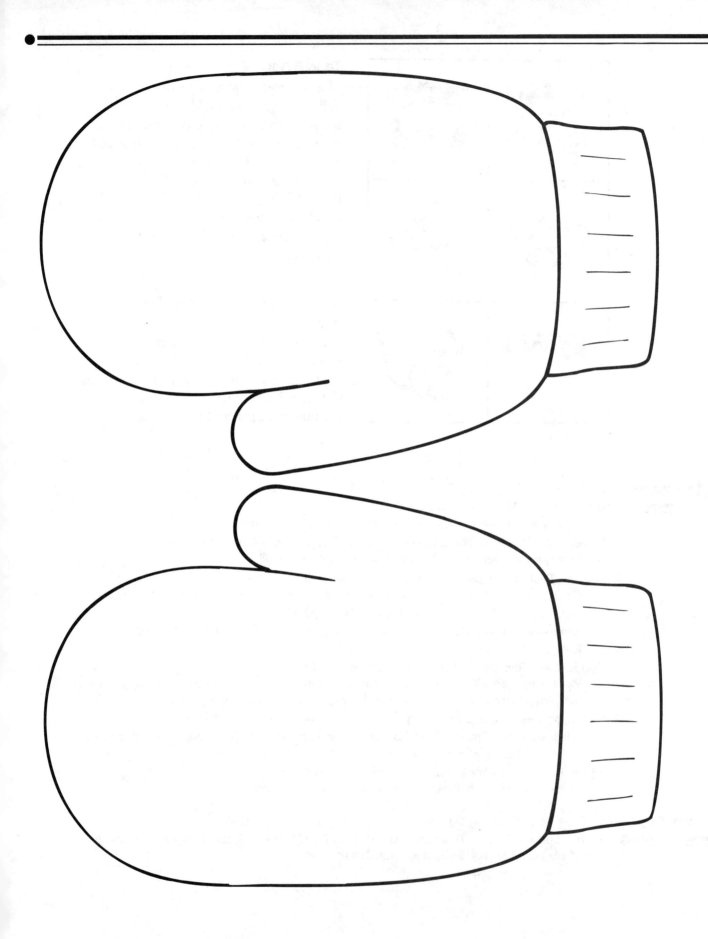

TLC10064 Copyright © Teaching & Learning Company, Carthage, IL 62321